MENTAL HEALTH MATTERS

UNDERSTANDING ANXIETY DISORDERS

AMY HOLT

ROSEN PUBLISHING

Published in 2026 by The Rosen Publishing Group, Inc.
2544 Clinton Street, Buffalo, NY 14224

Portions of this work were originally authored by Sheila Wyborny and published as *Anxiety Disorders*. All new material this edition authored by Amy Holt.

Editor: Jennifer Lombardo
Designer: Rachel Rising

Cataloging-in-Publication Data

Names: Holt, Amy.
Title: Understanding anxiety disorders / Amy Holt.
Description: First edition. | Buffalo, NY : Rosen Publishing, 2026. | Series: Mental health matters | Includes glossary and index.
Identifiers: ISBN 9781499479546 (pbk.) | ISBN 9781499479553 (library bound) | ISBN 9781499479560 (ebook)
Subjects: LCSH: Anxiety--Juvenile literature. | Anxiety disorders--Juvenile literature.
Classification: LCC BF575.A6 H65 2026 | DDC 152.4'6--dc23

Manufactured in the United States of America

CPSIA Compliance Information: Batch #CSRYA26. For further information, contact Rosen Publishing at 1-800-237-9932.

CONTENTS

FOREWORD

There are many misconceptions about illness, especially mental illness. Advances in scientific knowledge have increased our understanding of many diseases and disorders, including the common cold, diabetes, and cancer. Many of these sicknesses and chronic conditions cause physical symptoms that people can see and understand, and their causes are often easy to explain.

The same cannot always be said for mental illnesses. Mental disorders are just as common as physical disorders, but without physical symptoms, they are often dismissed. People tend to believe that a mental illness is easy to get over with enough willpower. They may call people with mental illnesses names such as "lazy" and "attention-seeking." Some people even deny that mental illnesses exist at all.

People who have been convinced by those around them that they have a problem of willpower rather than a treatable illness often go undiagnosed for years. This can cause a lot of suffering; people with an undiagnosed mental disorder often understand that they are experiencing the world in a different way than their peers, but they have no one to turn to for answers. Many feel guilty about not being able to control their symptoms, not realizing that this is as impractical as telling someone with a broken leg that they should be able to walk without pain if they simply try hard enough.

In recent years, the stigma, or perceived shame, of mental illness has decreased. More people, especially young people, are willing to seek therapy and talk openly about their diagnosed mental illnesses. However, this has also led to a rise in misinformation, which can be spread through personal anecdotes, social media, and even news sources. The misuse of "therapy speak" and armchair diagnoses by internet commenters are two growing problems. Furthermore, although the stigma has lessened, it has not disappeared completely. People sometimes use mental illnesses as insults. Someone who displays normal ranges of emotion, for example, may be called "bipolar" as an insult. This shows a lack of understanding about bipolar disorder and furthers the stigma around this disorder by making it sound like a negative aspect of who a person is.

This series aims to offer accurate information about mental illnesses so young adults will have a better understanding of them. Each volume discusses the symptoms of a particular illness, ways it is currently being treated, and the research that is being done to understand it further. Advice for people who may be suffering from a disorder is included, as well as information for their loved ones about how best to support them.

With fully cited quotes, a list of recommended books and websites for further research, and informational charts, this series provides young adults with a factual introduction to common mental illnesses. By learning more about these disorders, they will be better able to show compassion to people who are dealing with mental illnesses and take charge of their own mental health.

A STRESSFUL DISORDER

Anxiety and panic are normal feelings. Everyone has experienced them at one time or another, even if they do not have an anxiety disorder. Taking an important exam, giving a speech in front of a large crowd, or finding out that a loved one is in danger are all situations in which a person might experience anxiety or panic. Anxiety is a reaction humans developed to help them avoid danger. The primitive "fight or flight" responses were first experienced by ancient people when they faced possible danger. This feeling helped put them on alert until they could determine whether the perceived threat was real. For example, a rustle in the bushes could provoke an anxious reaction—a pounding heart, a rush of adrenaline, and heightened senses. If the rustle was followed by a leaping wolf, the person would be ready. If, instead,

Public speaking is a common source of anxiety.

a hedgehog crawled out of the bushes, the anxiety would subside. Even today, people respond to threats against their safety, welfare, or happiness with anxiety.

Anxiety is considered a disorder when a person experiences fear of things that most people would not find stressful or when that fear persists after the apparent cause is gone. In short, the body and mind react to normal things as if they were dangerous. People with panic disorder experience sudden, often unexplainable panic attacks—"sudden periods of intense fear that may include palpitations, pounding heart, or accelerated heart rate; sweating; trembling or shaking; sensations of shortness of breath, smothering, or choking; and feeling of impending doom."[1]

Because the term "anxiety" can be used to describe either mild or severe feelings of distress and fear, anxiety disorders have historically not been well understood by the general public. In recent years, people have been attempting to raise awareness of the seriousness of these disorders and how they differ from the normal nervousness that everyone experiences from time to time.

Anxiety is not one disorder, but several. Social anxiety, generalized anxiety, agoraphobia, specific phobias, and panic disorder are all types of anxiety disorders. Someone may have just one of these, or they may have several. Anxiety disorders are extremely common; according to the National Institute of Mental Health (NIMH), about 19 percent of American adults are affected by one or more of them.

AN OLD DISORDER

People of any race, ethnic group, religion, or income level can be affected by anxiety disorders. People from the past also lived with anxiety disorders, although formal diagnoses of mental illnesses were not available until modern times. Because doctors did not understand anxiety and its causes for much of history, their treatments were often bizarre and did not work. A poet named Alfred, Lord Tennyson, once described his feelings of extreme panic and anxiety and his hopes for improvement shortly before he began a controversial—and ultimately ineffective—treatment program of wet sheets and cold baths: "The perpetual panic and horror of the last two years had steeped my nerves in poison: now I am left a beggar but am or shall be shortly somewhat better off in nerves."[2] Despite this treatment and others, he continued to experience what was then called "nervous illness" throughout his life.

Charlotte Brontë, another important writer, suffered from similar disorders. Brontë, the author of

Treatment methods for anxiety disorders have come a long way since Charlotte Brontë's time.

Jane Eyre, was troubled by periods of anxiety and depression. Treatments to improve her condition were also unsuccessful. For instance, she was treated with oral doses of mercury, a poisonous metal. The only effect this had was to make her violently ill.

As the fields of medicine and psychology have progressed, doctors are more aware of what causes anxiety and how to treat it, although it is still not fully understood. More research must be done in the future to gain an even stronger understanding of the various anxiety disorders and how to help those living with them.

Anxiety disorders can be difficult for people to deal with in their daily lives. They can interfere with normal tasks such as sleeping, leaving the house, and interacting with other people. Some people can overcome their anxiety disorder by seeing a therapist and making some life changes, especially if the anxiety is mild or has an obvious cause, such as a bad living situation. Others need both therapy and medication. Medication can be very helpful when the anxiety is severe or is caused by a chemical imbalance in the brain. The use of medication for mental illnesses is often stigmatized, but medical professionals see it as a tool to help people, much like medication is often used to help people with a chronic physical condition or illness.

WHAT IS ANXIETY?

In many situations, anxiety is a helpful response the brain has evolved to keep us safe by warning us that something is not right. For instance, if a child is playing outside and a loud thunderstorm can be heard in the distance, they may feel anxious and run inside where it is safe. If the child does not have an anxiety disorder, their feelings of fear will go away shortly after they get inside and away from the storm. In some cases, though, a child may continue to feel intense anxiety about the storm even after being told that they are safe inside their house. They may worry excessively about when the next storm will come or lose sleep because they are too afraid that they will be woken up by a thunderstorm. In these cases, the severity of the anxiety might signal a disorder.

By definition, anxiety disorders are a group of abnormal fears and nervous conditions. Often, the thing that triggers an anxiety or panic attack is not real or dangerous. For instance, someone who is perfectly healthy may worry excessively that they actually have some kind of illness, even when a doctor assures them that they are healthy. Sometimes this type of worry can occur with no visible cause; someone may have no idea why they are anxious. However, this often makes the feelings harder to deal with, as the person cannot identify what their mind is trying to alert them to.

Anxiety can cause headaches, nausea, and other physcial symptoms.

Anxiety disorders can range from mild to extreme. For instance, one person with a phobia of spiders may go out of their way to avoid walking near a spider, while another person with the same phobia may have a panic attack if they even see a picture of a spider. These disorders also have a variety of causes. Biologically, anxiety disorders can be caused by abnormalities in brain chemistry or side effects from an illness or drug. They can be inherited—passed down from parent to child biologically—or triggered by stressful events in a person's life. Whatever the cause, though, anxiety disorders in their extreme states can seriously interfere with a person's life. They can get in the way of family relationships and affect careers.

Anxiety disorders have been classified according to specific behavioral characteristics. The following are some of the most common ones experienced by teenagers and adults today. In addition, information is provided about two disorders that used to be classified as anxiety disorders but were given new distinctions by experts in recent years. These disorders often feature extreme anxiety as a common symptom.

GENERALIZED ANXIETY DISORDER

According to the Anxiety and Depression Association of America (ADAA), generalized anxiety disorder (GAD) sufferers account for about 3.1 percent of all people who suffer from anxiety disorders. GAD is characterized by constant worries and fears, which can get in the way of a person's ability to function normally on a daily basis. GAD sufferers are almost always anxious about something, and they might not even know why. They may feel generally restless and anxious about nearly anything, and their symptoms are difficult or impossible to control. They worry excessively about things such as their job, their health, their family, their relationships, and the weather, and they often catastrophize, or think of the worst-case scenario in any situation. For instance, if a person with GAD is hired for a new job, they might worry that they will make a mistake and be fired. Even if their boss praises them for their work, they may still be on high alert for any possible mistakes. If they do make a mistake, no matter how minor, they often panic and see it as worse than it is. To someone with GAD, putting a comma in the wrong place can feel as disastrous as losing an entire file full of important paperwork. Their anxiety can be increased if their boss treats minor mistakes as huge ones.

People with GAD tend to feel "keyed up" most of the time and have difficulty concentrating on any subject. Sometimes, their minds simply go blank. They often have trouble sleeping, suffer from headaches, and experience muscle tension or pain, especially in the back, shoulders, and neck. In moments of intense stress, GAD can produce symptoms such as sweating, nausea, dizziness, and the need to make frequent trips to the bathroom. Fatigue, or extreme tiredness, is another symptom. People may feel fatigued because they are unable to sleep at night, and after suffering a period of intense anxiety known as a panic attack or anxiety attack, they may feel exhausted because intense fear uses up a lot of the body's energy to keep people alert and ready to respond to any possible danger.

GAD can cause exhaustion by making it difficult to sleep.

Many people suffering from GAD use defense mechanisms to cope with their problems. Some may try to hide or disguise the condition. Some blame others for their anxieties. A young person with GAD may say teachers and other students are picking on them and causing their worries or blame a sibling for their feelings. An adult might say their boss has it in for them. They may express their anxiety as anger.

Denial is another defense mechanism. The person may tell others that they have no problem with anxiety. They might even deny it to themselves. People who use these defense mechanisms are not actually dealing with their problems, though. They are merely putting off facing their condition and getting help for it. In fact, the ADAA estimates that only about 43 percent of GAD sufferers are actually getting the help they need. This can be harmful for them and their loved ones because when someone is in denial, they convince themselves that their fears are completely logical and rational. This may lead to fights with friends and family when loved ones try to tell the person that the thing they are worrying about is not likely to happen.

One person described a period of time when their GAD was at its worst:

> *I'd have terrible sleeping problems. There were times I'd wake up wired in the middle of the night. I had trouble concentrating, even reading the newspaper or a novel. Sometimes I'd feel a little lightheaded. My heart would race or pound. And that would make me worry more. I was always imagining things were worse than they really were: when I got a stomachache, I'd think it was an ulcer.*[3]

People who have GAD do not typically avoid situations the way people with other anxiety disorders might. Often, they understand that their worries are out of proportion to the situation, and when the anxiety passes, they realize that there was nothing threatening about that particular situation after all. For this reason, it is common for people with GAD to feel intense guilt or shame about their anxiety attacks, even though it is not their fault they have those feelings. Mental disorders make certain feelings difficult or impossible to control without therapy or medication, and it is not the sufferer's fault that they have a disorder.

Frequently, GAD starts in childhood or adolescence and gets worse slowly over time. It can come on so slowly that sometimes the person is not aware of the condition until it is seriously affecting their daily life. A diagnosis of GAD is generally made after the person seeking help has been in a state of excessive worry for about six months. In a mild state, people with GAD can function normally in everyday life, but in extreme cases, a person may have difficulty getting through even the most mundane situations without catastrophizing and feeling intense anxiety.

PHOBIAS

Of all the anxiety disorders, phobias may be the most common. In fact, many experts believe that specific phobia, or fear of a specific thing, is the most common type of mental disorder in the United States. An estimated 9.1 percent of American adults suffer from at least one phobia, according to the NIMH. Many people fear certain objects or situations, but when these fears become so extreme that they interfere with daily activities, they are classified as a phobia. A medical diagnosis of phobia is generally made when a person has experienced symptoms for six months or more. Some people are affected by two or more phobias at the same time. Phobias involve intense, irrational, or unexplainable fears.

These fears can be associated with objects, animals, insects, people, situations, or places. Most phobias are associated with things that pose little or no danger to the person experiencing the phobia.

No matter how cute or friendly a dog is, it can be very scary to a person with a phobia of dogs.

A person does not even have to be in the presence of the source of their phobia to trigger it. Seeing the object of their fear in a picture or on television—or even thinking about it—is often enough to cause a reaction.

Specific phobias can be broken down into several categories. Animal phobia is the fear of animals or insects. Natural environment phobias involve a fear of things such as storms, heights, darkness, or water. People who have an abnormal fear of blood, getting injections, or being injured suffer from blood-injection-injury type phobia. Situational type phobias can be triggered by different types of transportation, such as automobiles, airplanes, or buses, or enclosed places such as tunnels or elevators.

A fear of heights, flying, being in a small space, snakes, and insects are common specific phobias, but people can also have phobic reactions to something as nonthreatening as balloons, a type of vegetable, pencils, chalk, or even certain numbers. Both children and adults with unusual specific phobias are often teased and laughed at, but phobias are no laughing matter. Like any mental disorder, if they are severe enough, they can seriously disrupt a person's life, put jobs at risk, and damage or destroy relationships.

ANXIETY IN SOCIAL SITUATIONS

Although social anxiety disorder (SAD) is also called social phobia, it is different than a specific phobia. People with social anxiety are afraid of being embarrassed or criticized or attracting some other type of negative attention in public places or situations. They often fear things such as speaking in public, talking on the phone, or interacting with cashiers. This can make

For some people, making a phone call is a minor task. For people with social anxiety, it can spark panic.

it difficult for them to perform everyday tasks that most people have no trouble with, such as making a dentist appointment or going grocery shopping. They often avoid parties and other group events, as well as crowded places such as shopping malls and theaters. Like those who deal with other kinds of anxiety disorders, those with SAD experience anxiety so severe that it interferes with their everyday life.

People with this type of anxiety may come across as shy and introverted. They may not look people in the eye when they speak with them. However, others may hide their discomfort well enough that no one can see it. Not everyone with anxiety reacts the same way to all situations, so it can sometimes come as a surprise to people when they find out that someone they know has an anxiety disorder such as SAD.

AVOIDING PLACES

Like SAD, agoraphobia is distinct from specific phobias. Agoraphobia is a complex anxiety disorder. It is characterized by extreme fear and anxiety associated with being in a particular place or a situation. Often, people with this disorder avoid places where they have already had a panic attack; for instance, if someone has a panic attack while they are grocery shopping, they may begin to order their groceries online to avoid going to a grocery store again. According to the ADAA, people with agoraphobia

> *typically avoid public places where they feel immediate escape might be difficult, such as shopping malls, public transportation, or large sports arenas. About one in three people with panic disorder develops agoraphobia … Some people develop a fixed route or territory, and it may become impossible for them to travel beyond their safety zones without suffering severe anxiety.*[4]

In the past, agoraphobia was considered a type of panic disorder. However, in the latest edition of the book mental health professionals use to diagnose people, the *Diagnostic and Statistical Manual of Mental Disorders, 5th Edition* (*DSM-5*), it has been reclassified as its own anxiety disorder.

BREAKING THE SILENCE

Historically, anxiety disorders have not been well understood by people who do not experience them, but awareness and acceptance of anxiety has been growing as more people speak out about their struggles. Celebrities, in particular, have been an important part of decreasing the stigma around anxiety. Because they are so often in the spotlight, they have generally learned how to hide their anxiety, so speaking out about it shows people that anyone can have an anxiety disorder. Emma Stone, Beyoncé, Adele, Chris Evans, Shawn Mendes, and many others have publicly discussed their anxiety. Actress Kristen Bell (*right*) has been particularly outspoken about the fact that anxiety and depression are not causes for shame, even if someone needs medication to control them. In an article for *Motto* magazine, she said:

> *It's a knee-jerk reaction to judge people when they're vulnerable. But there's nothing weak about struggling with mental illness. You're just having a harder time living in your brain than other people. And I don't want you to feel alone ... Talking about how you're feeling is the first step to helping yourself.*[1]

1. Kristen Bell, "Kristen Bell: I'm Over Staying Silent About Depression," *Motto*, May 31, 2016. motto.time.com/4352130/kristen-bell-frozen-depression-anxiety/.

This change came about because mental health professionals have found that some people with agoraphobia do not experience panic attacks. People who have agoraphobia without panic disorder typically avoid places because they have certain specific phobias, such as fear of experiencing a crime or terrorist attack, fear of getting a contagious disease from someone they encounter in a public space, or fear of embarrassing themselves in public.

PANIC DISORDER

Panic attacks are often associated with anxiety disorders. People who have panic attacks are overcome with fear and experience physical symptoms such as shortness of breath, rapid heartbeat, trembling, choking, numbness in the hands, and nausea. They may also have a feeling of "going crazy;" a feeling of things being unreal, like being in a dream; and a need to escape the situation they are in. It is not uncommon for people to believe they are having a heart attack the first time they experience a panic attack.

Possibly the worst thing about panic attacks and panic disorders is that people have no control over when they will occur. They can come on suddenly with little or no warning and are terrifying. Panic attacks typically last between five and twenty minutes, but to the person who is experiencing one, they can feel endless. In between attacks, they often think obsessively about when the next one will occur and what to do when it happens.

Panic disorder affects 2 to 3 percent of adult Americans. However, not everyone who has panic attacks will develop panic disorder. It is possible for people to have just one panic attack and then never experience another. In fact, about one in three adult Americans will experience one panic attack at some time in their lives. Panic attacks become panic disorder when the symptoms, or obsessive worry about those symptoms, persist for a month or more. If left untreated, panic disorder can become a severe

Many comedians, such as Maria Bamford (*shown here*), have spoken openly about anxiety and panic.

disability. Since some of the symptoms are the same as those of a heart attack, people may make several trips to the emergency room or see a number of doctors before the condition is correctly diagnosed.

One person who experienced these attacks described this fear: "In between attacks there is this dread and anxiety that it's going to happen again. I'm afraid to go back to places where I've had an attack. Unless I get help, there soon won't be any place where I can go and feel safe from panic."[5]

WHAT ABOUT OCD?

Obsessive-compulsive disorder (OCD) is similar to anxiety disorders. In fact, for many years, it was classified as an anxiety disorder. Today, however, it has its own medical classification. Despite being seen as a separate disorder, it is helpful to look at OCD alongside anxiety disorders because of their shared symptoms. For example, a person with OCD may be obsessed with troublesome thoughts or worries that prey on the mind and sometimes prevent the person from functioning normally. For instance, someone may have a persistent fear that a door has been left unlocked so burglars might get in, or that the stove or the coffeemaker has been left on, which might start a fire and burn down the house. Some OCD sufferers fear harming someone or catching a serious disease.

The other half of this disorder is compulsion. People with OCD have intrusive, or unwanted and distressing, thoughts that they find impossible to dismiss until they have performed certain rituals, or repetitive behaviors. Repeated hand washing, leaving and entering a room a certain number of times, or turning lights on and off a certain number of times are well-known and highly visible examples of compulsive behavior, but less obvious compulsions can include things such as repeated online searches or asking for reassurance from another person. The person fears that something bad will happen if these rituals are not performed, or they may perform the rituals to make a bad feeling go away. The compulsive behavior relieves the bad feeling, but only temporarily. When the anxiety returns, the person will feel compelled to perform the ritualistic behavior again. It becomes a self-destructive cycle.

One OCD sufferer described how intense some of his compulsions became: "I switched the light switch on and off at least a hundred times. I would check under my bed every night. I checked the zipper on my pants to see if it was open. I always checked the back of my jacket to see if anyone had put a sticker on it. I was very paranoid and felt insecure. I also washed my hands more than needed."[6] In order to be diagnosed as OCD, the rituals must take up a lot of time or cause distress in social or work situations. In other words, someone who double-checks that a door is locked probably does not have OCD, but someone who will not leave the house until they have locked and unlocked the door 20 times, or who leaves work several times a day to check that the stove has not somehow turned itself on while they were gone, probably does.

One type of OCD that is harder to diagnose is called primarily cognitive (or primarily obsessional) obsessive-compulsive disorder, sometimes nicknamed "pure-O." In this form of the disorder, sufferers have intrusive thoughts that they obsess over, but few or no outwardly observable rituals. Instead, they create rituals inside their heads, such as repeating a certain phrase over and over or counting to a certain number. Thinking about the thoughts obsessively is a type of ritual; they may ask themselves over and over again, 'What is the proof that I would not do this?' They may also look for outside reassurance, often by googling questions such as, "How can I tell if I'm a psychopath?" Many people with OCD have a mix of physical and mental compulsions; pure-O is rare, and some experts question whether it exists because there is debate over whether some compulsions, such as checking and reassurance-seeking, should be classified as physical or mental.

The fear that accompanies intrusive thoughts leads people with OCD to believe that there must be something wrong with them for having the thought. OCD sufferers who experience intrusive thoughts are generally scared to tell anyone about them because of how unsettling the thoughts can be. They may believe they are secretly pedophiles, or murderers, or they have other thoughts about themselves that they find distressing. In reality, though, they would never act on these thoughts. In fact, intrusive thoughts are often the exact opposite of the sufferer's values, which is what makes them so distressing. All people experience intrusive thoughts on occasion. However, people with OCD are unable to let the thought go and instead experience intense anxiety surrounding the thought and what it means.

Intrusive thoughts are not always about things that society views as being wrong; they may simply be things that the person feels would change their personality or be difficult for them to deal with. For instance, someone from a Christian family may worry that they are secretly an atheist.

OCD compulsions only bring relief for a short amount of time. When the fear comes in again, the person repeats the compulsion. Over time, the compulsions can start to take over a person's life and become a source of distress themselves.

OCD is marked by a desire for certainty that cannot be fulfilled. The rituals people perform and reassurance they seek only reinforce the belief that their intrusive thoughts are something to be feared, and like a drug, the OCD sufferer becomes dependent on the rituals and reassurance. According to the International OCD Foundation, the thought process of someone with OCD goes something like this:

> *I must always have certainty and control in life … I must be in control of all my thoughts and emotions at all times. If I lose control of my thoughts, I must do something to regain that control. Thinking the thought means it is important, and it is important because I think about it. It is abnormal to have intrusive thoughts, and if I do have them it means I'm crazy, weird, etc. Having an intrusive thought and doing what it suggests are the same thing morally. Thinking about doing harm, and not preventing it, is just as bad as committing harm … Having intrusive thoughts means I am likely to act on them. I cannot take the risk that my thoughts will come true.*[7]

INTRUSIVE VS. IMPULSIVE

A common phrase in memes and TikToks is, "I let my intrusive thoughts win." This is typically used in a joking manner to describe things such as a person cutting their bangs, redecorating an entire room in one day, or cutting a long shirt into a crop top. However, this is a misunderstanding of intrusive thoughts, which are always unwanted and distressing. A sudden fun or silly thought is an impulsive thought.

While both intrusive and impulsive thoughts pop into a person's head suddenly, the difference between them is that intrusive thoughts are upsetting. They frequently center on violence or on disregarding social norms. For example, a person may have an intrusive thoughts about swerving their car into oncoming traffic while driving or taking all their clothes off in the middle of math class. The idea of acting on such thoughts is scary, not funny. Using the word "intrusive" to describe impulsive thoughts makes people feel even more ashamed of their actual intrusive thoughts. A social media star named Kris Collins, who goes by kallmekris on YouTube and TikTok, has made several videos to help people understand the difference between the two kinds of thoughts.

In contrast, people without OCD generally recognize that their thoughts wander and that sometimes a random, possibly bizarre thought will pop into their heads. They are often able to dismiss it without fear.

Over time, as mental health professionals study anxiety disorders, they learn that what they thought in the past is not always true. For example, hoarding disorder used to be considered a sub-type of OCD, but it is now considered a separate disorder. A person with hoarding disorder, sometimes referred to as a "hoarder," feels compelled to collect and save things. Many of these items are totally useless, such as broken dishes or appliances that cannot be repaired. Hanging on to materials, such as old magazines, newspapers, or junk mail, until they fill large spaces in the home and become a health or fire hazard, is a potentially dangerous compulsion.

Although OCD is no longer classified as an anxiety disorder, it still causes feelings of extreme anxiety in those who suffer from it.

Many people with this disorder simply cannot bring themselves to get rid of anything. Purchasing items far beyond what is needed or can be used is also a form of hoarding. For instance, instead of purchasing a six-roll package of paper towels and then going back to the store and buying more when they run out, the hoarder might buy two or three cases of paper towels, bathroom tissue, or cleaning products and stack them in the corner of the dining room or the garage. Although hoarding is compulsive behavior, people with hoarding disorder do not show any other signs of OCD, which is why it has been reclassified. The difficulty in distinguishing between a person with OCD who has a compulsion to hoard things and a person with hoarding disorder can cause people to be misdiagnosed and, therefore, not properly treated.

Some compulsive behaviors involve trying to be perfect, trying to do things perfectly, or trying to create a perfect environment. These compulsive behaviors include excessive cleaning or ordering and arranging items in the environment. People who are obsessed with being perfect or doing things perfectly might keep new purchases unused and in their original packages for months or years. They may avoid using closets or rooms once they have been perfectly arranged or feel a need to arrange items in storage in a certain order—for instance, arranging the cans on the pantry shelf in pairs or symmetrical arrangements. They may become upset if someone moves the items without asking.

At one time, OCD was thought to be a relatively rare disorder. In the 1950s, only about 0.05 percent of adult Americans were diagnosed with it. Since then, though, the numbers have grown. In fact, by 1985, that figure had increased to 2.5 percent, and, according to studies done by Columbia University Medical Center and Villanova University, OCD sufferers currently make up about 2.3 percent of the adult population in the United States, or about 1 in 40 people.

ANXIETY AND PTSD

Like OCD, PTSD was once considered an anxiety disorder but is now classified in a separate category of mental illnesses. However, extreme anxiety is a part of this disorder's symptoms, so it is often studied alongside other disorders that cause intense feelings of worry, such as OCD and anxiety disoders. PTSD generally results from a potentially life-threatening trauma, such as physical or sexual assault. PTSD can also be brought on by a natural disaster, such as a hurricane, a tornado, a fire, or a flood. People in the military, particularly those returning from combat duty, are especially at risk for this condition.

People suffering from PTSD tend to avoid things that remind them of the experiences that caused the condition. Often, they do not wish to talk about or even think about these events. People with PTSD may become reclusive, avoiding family, friends, and activities that they once enjoyed.

People with PTSD may relive the traumatic event that caused their condition in several ways. They may have upsetting thoughts that intrude into their daily lives or suffer from recurring nightmares. In some cases, people with PTSD experience what are called flashbacks—vivid memories of traumatic events. A person experiencing a flashback may have the feeling of reliving the traumatic event. Flashbacks can be triggered by the anniversary of the traumatic event, as well as certain sounds, smells, or seemingly innocent activities, such as children playing tag on a playground. Sometimes, the flashbacks occur with no triggers. The person experiencing the flashback can become extremely agitated and disoriented. These periods can last from a few minutes to many hours.

The news media began doing reports on PTSD and flashbacks in the late 1960s and early 1970s, when some soldiers returning from combat in the Vietnam War were diagnosed with the disorder, which was called "shell shock" at the time. It was named for the bombs, or shells, that were dropped during wars. It was later renamed when mental health professionals realized PTSD could be caused by much more than bombs. The soldiers with PTSD were unable to let go of the horrors of battle and its aftermath, and the persistent thoughts affected many of them psychologically. A child crying on a playground could trigger memories of Vietnamese children crying for their dead parents. The sound of a firecracker could send soldiers mentally back to the scene of a battle. Psychiatric services at veterans' facilities throughout the country have personnel trained to work with PTSD patients.

PTSD is classified as acute when the symptoms have been affecting the patient for less than three months and chronic when the symptoms have continued for more than three months. Sometimes, symptoms do not begin immediately after the traumatic event. One symptom is a drastic change in personality. For instance, a generally calm person may become restless or irritable. They may begin avoiding friends and family as well as situations that trigger reminders of the traumatic event. They may experience a feeling of hypervigilance, or always being on the lookout for potential threats, never able to relax. If and when these symptoms appear, it is important for them to get help.

MULTIPLE ANXIETY DISORDERS

A comorbidity is when a person has two or more diseases at the same time. Depression and substance abuse, which are each classified as mental disorders

Taking prescription drugs can help with anxiety disorders. However, abusing prescription drugs causes even more problems. Always discuss medications with a doctor.

according to the *DSM-5*, are common comorbidities of anxiety disorders. Depression can occur as a result of chemical changes in the brain similar to the ones that cause anxiety, or it can occur as a reaction to a situation. For instance, the death of a loved one or stress at school can cause depression, which is characterized by feelings of sadness, emptiness, and hopelessness. People with depression often lose interest in things they formerly enjoyed doing and may think about suicide if the situation is severe or goes on for a long time.

People who are experiencing anxiety or depression may begin to drink alcohol or abuse drugs as a way to escape their feelings. Sometimes they may not even realize that what they are doing is a problem until they are addicted. Alcohol and prescription drugs are two of the most abused substances in the United States, and they are often taken by people who are trying to self-medicate instead of seeking professional help. Self-medication is dangerous because drugs and alcohol have serious side effects in addition to the risk of addiction.

People who self-medicate often do so because they are unwilling or unable to seek help. Although more awareness has been brought to anxiety in recent years, many people still feel a stigma around seeing a therapist. They may believe that only people with serious mental illnesses see therapists, and they may also try to tell themselves that their own anxiety is not serious and that they can handle it on their own. However, they are often in denial about how bad their situation is.

Other people may not seek help because of the cost. In the United States, there are many complex factors that go into health insurance prices and coverage, but most people agree that insurance prices are higher than the average American can afford, even if an employer is paying part of the premium, or monthly cost. Prices are higher than in any other developed country in the world, and many insurance plans set limits on what is covered.

Many insurance plans cover prescription medications but do not cover therapy to treat mental illness or stress. Even when they do, many therapists do not accept insurance because they find the insurance system difficult and confusing to manage. For this reason, people may not seek therapy because they feel they are unable to afford it. However, some therapists offer treatment on a sliding scale, meaning that they charge what the client can afford. Research into therapy takes some time and effort, but people who have benefited from treatment say that it is well worth it.

It is not unusual for people to try to hide perceived weaknesses or even deny problems altogether, but a person experiencing one or more anxiety disorders needs to understand that this is a potentially serious mental condition, not something shameful that needs to be hidden. The person should seek help, rather than trying to hide the condition. Like the flu or any other physical illness, without the right kind of medical help, anxiety disorders can become much worse. Not taking the proper steps to treat these conditions can result in poor performance at school; loss of employment, friendships, and family relationships; and, in the worst cases, loss of people's lives.

MYTHS AND FACTS

In the past, anxiety was not recognized as a mental illness; it was sometimes seen as a sign of weakness, laziness, or self-absorption. Women have always tended to be diagnosed with anxiety more often than men, which led many people—even doctors, for a long time—to believe that women were weak, hysterical, and could not control their emotions. Because people did not know what anxiety was, they saw it as a personality flaw rather than a legitimate mental illness.

As society advanced, more became known about the human brain and how mental illness can change the way it functions. However, many people still have misconceptions, or false ideas, about anxiety disorders. The idea of someone being "crazy" has an enormous stigma surrounding it, and many people—even ones who suffer from their own form of mental illness—are afraid of or disgusted by people with mental illnesses. It is important for people to learn the truth about anxiety disorders and other mental illnesses so society can begin to change its views and behavior.

MYTH: "YOU'RE TOO YOUNG TO HAVE A MENTAL ILLNESS"

Some adults believe that because children and teens have fewer responsibilities, they also have fewer problems. However, mental health professionals know this is untrue. According to the Centers for Disease

Control and Prevention (CDC), about 10 percent of children ages 3 to 17 have at least one anxiety disorder. Of that 10 percent, 9 percent were male and 11 percent were female.

Although people of any age can suffer from any anxiety disorder, certain types are more common among people of specific age groups. For instance, phobias tend to appear before age nine. In addition, certain anxiety disorders are more likely to affect children rather than adults. These include separation anxiety and selective mutism, which is is an anxiety disorder that causes someone to be unable to speak in certain situations, despite being able to speak well in others.

One issue, especially among young children, is that they may not be able to clearly describe how they are feeling, so it is harder for doctors to make a diagnosis. For this reason, anxiety disorders in children may be overlooked or misdiagnosed. These children may become frustrated because they cannot make people understand what they are feeling. Sometimes, their frustration causes them to act out, both at school and at home.

Phobias are common among young children. Many children are afraid of the dark, especially dark rooms, the dark spaces under beds, and closets. It is fairly common for parents to make quick checks under beds and in closets to assure their young children that there are no monsters lurking. Often, children grow out of these fears; however, sometimes they become serious. If these fears trouble a child on a regular basis or appear to become more extreme, parents should consider seeking medical help for their child.

Some of the anxiety disorders that tend to appear when people reach their teens or 20s are GAD, SAD,

WHAT ARE YOU SO AFRAID OF?

percentage of Americans who say they fear...

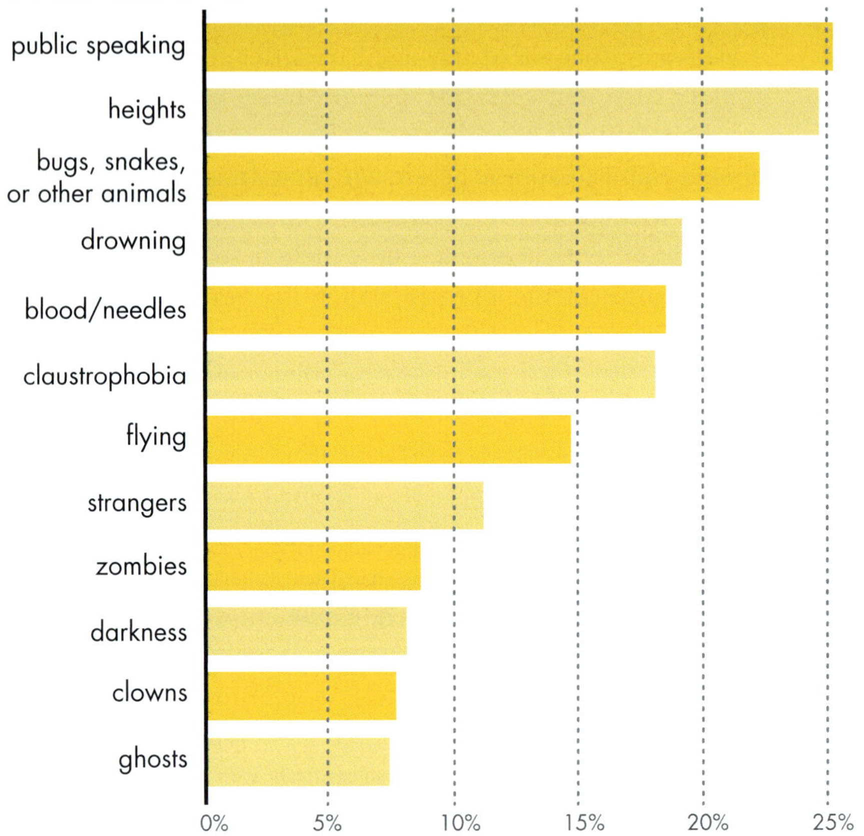

Some phobias are very common, as this information from the *Washington Post* shows.

panic disorder, and agoraphobia. As with adults, GAD in teens is characterized by excessive worry and anxiety about many different things. For young people, these worries revolve around such issues as grades; their performance in sports, music, or plays; being on time for classes and clubs; family problems; their health; relationships with their friends; and climate change, as well as other issues.

Young people with GAD suffer from physical symptoms such as irritability, fatigue, insomnia, restlessness, and general muscle tension. These teens tend to be perfectionists. They may redo school reports or projects several times and still not be satisfied with their work. They constantly seek approval from others and are often hard on themselves.

Teens with SAD have difficulty engaging others in conversation, speaking in front of their classes, making plans with friends, or doing any sort of performances in front of groups, such as plays, skits, debating, or singing. This condition affects the quality of their school experiences and personal relationships.

People with social anxiety may appear unfriendly and unwilling to get to know people. However, most avoid others out of fear that they will make a social mistake, not because they dislike other people.

One consequence of SAD is that sufferers tend to isolate themselves from others. Because it is so difficult for them to reach out to people they do not know well, they may develop a reputation among their classmates for being snobby, standoffish, or rude. However, the truth is that they often want to be sociable and reach out to form friendships, but they are too anxious to do so. This leaves them feeling lonely, which may contribute to depression and substance abuse. When they do make friends, they may ask for reassurance over and over again that they are not bothering their friends by asking to hang out with them. This can be frustrating for friends, so it is important for both the person with SAD and their friends to work together to strike a balance between constant assurance and no assurance at all.

Panic disorder tends to appear between the ages of 15 and 25, and people who develop agoraphobia as a result will typically see those symptoms about six months after developing panic disorder. Agoraphobia without panic disorder generally appears before age 27.

Under the best of conditions, the teen years can be difficult. Many young people have not yet developed a strong sense of self-worth or self-confidence. Additionally, many teens dread doing anything other teens would find socially unacceptable. Peer acceptance is one of the top teen priorities, and increased hormone activity can result in crying episodes or temper eruptions over relatively minor issues. When an anxiety disorder is added to this mix, the results can be overwhelming and can have lasting effects on a young person's life. If any sort of disorder is suspected, the young person should tell a trusted adult, such as a family member or guidance counselor, in order to receive the proper help.

MYTH: "MEN ARE MORE LOGICAL AND THEREFORE LESS ANXIOUS THAN WOMEN"

Various studies indicate that at least twice as many women are affected by anxiety disorders than men. Some people believe this is because men are better at controlling their emotions than women. However, research has shown this is untrue. Some researchers believe the difference comes from brain chemistry.

WHAT DOES IT FEEL LIKE?

People who deal with anxiety disorders often struggle to describe what it feels like. Because everyone deals with anxiety at some point, it is sometimes difficult for people without the disorder to understand how hard it is for someone with the disorder to dismiss their anxious thoughts and feelings, even when they know they are irrational. Comedian Maria Bamford described her anxiety in a humorous way:

> *This is what my anxiety feels like: It's like we're at a wonderful party, just a regular party, everybody's having a good time; and then all of a sudden somebody shows up in a pretty frighteningly realistic Dracula costume. And ... everyone says, "Oh yeah, it's [just] Steve ..." But he won't say he's Steve ... And then he starts chasing you. That's what I feel like all the time.*[1]

Other people have also attempted to describe how their anxiety feels in a way that people who do not experience it constantly can try to understand:

> *Anxiety is the mini heart attack you receive when you're walking down the stairs and miss a step, but your heart never calms down and the butterflies remain in the pit of your stomach.*
>
> *Anxiety [constantly feels like] when you are watching a scary movie and you know something is about to pop out and scare you, but it never does, so you just keep waiting for it to happen ...*
>
> *Anxiety is feeling like [everyday] tasks, such as taking a shower, might result in your harm, even though reality tries to convince you otherwise.*[2]

1. "Stay Alive Out of Spite," YouTube video, 2:07, posted by Maria Bamford—Topic, November 11, 2016. www.youtube.com/watch?v=o_dOFmmJLZ4.

2. Julia Vachon, "9 Metaphors That Describe Anxiety to Non-Anxious People," *Odyssey*, August 8, 2016. www.theodysseyonline.com/9-metaphors-describe-anxiety-anxious-people.

According to the ADAA:

> *The brain system involved in the fight-or-flight response is activated more readily in women and*

stays activated longer than men, partly as a result of the action of estrogen and progesterone.

The neurotransmitter serotonin may also play a role in responsiveness to stress and anxiety. Some evidence suggests that the female brain does not process serotonin as quickly as the male brain. Recent research has found that women are more sensitive to low levels of corticotropin-releasing factor (CRF), a hormone that organizes stress responses in mammals, making them twice as vulnerable as men to stress-related disorders.[8]

Those who experience menstruation, or getting a period, are also affected by the hormones associated with that. Many experience premenstrual syndrome (PMS), a condition that happens a few days before their period starts. It is common for people with PMS to feel sad, angry, or anxious over things that would not normally upset them. These symptoms are generally mild, last only a few days, and go away after the period

PMS can cause intense physical and emotional changes. The emotional symptoms can be very difficult to control.

starts. However, about 1.6 percent of menstruating people experience a condition called premenstrual dysphoric disorder (PMDD). That works out to about 31 million people worldwide. Researchers note that because the symptoms need to be present for at least six months before a person can be diagnosed, there are likely many more people who have PMDD but do not know it yet.

PMDD is a form of PMS that lasts longer and has more severe symptoms, some of which can seriously disrupt a woman's daily life. Symptoms include intense, uncontrollable anger; depression characterized by feelings of hopelessness and sometimes suicidal thoughts; mood swings; anxiety; difficulty concentrating; changes in appetite; and changes in sleep patterns (suddenly sleeping too much or too little). These symptoms begin when a person who is born biologically female starts ovulating—when a their body releases an egg—and last up to two weeks, when they begin their period. In order for doctors to know that it is PMDD and not a different illness unrelated to menstruation, this person must have at least seven days each month when they do not experience symptoms. Researchers are not sure exactly what causes PMDD, but they believe lower than normal levels of serotonin may be to blame. PMS and PMDD can cause severe anxiety, and they can also make an existing anxiety disorder worse.

Additionally, more women than men suffer from specific phobias, panic disorder, and agoraphobia. Men and women are about equal with regard to SAD; however, some studies put the numbers slightly higher among men.

Although hormonal differences do play a part in the difference between the number of men and women who experience anxiety, some professionals believe that the disparity, or difference, can sometimes be attributed to problems with diagnosis. A study by the American Psychological Association (APA) found that more women than men were diagnosed with PTSD even when both study participants had gone through similar traumatic events.

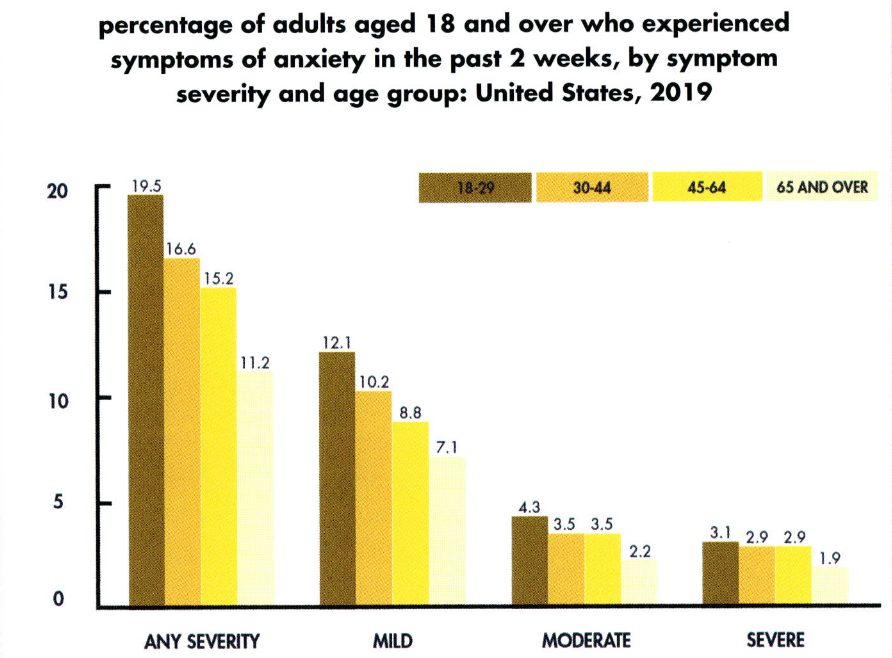

This information from the CDC shows that young adults tend to report experiencing symptoms of anxiety in larger numbers than older adults.

The researchers believe this may be because currently, the symptoms used to diagnose PTSD are exhibited more by women than men. Male study participants "were less likely to report anxiety or depression, but were more likely to report behavior and drug problems. They were also more likely to become irritable, angry or violent after traumas."[9] A change in the diagnostic criteria may help more men identify and treat their PTSD.

Panic disorder in men is also more likely to be misdiagnosed, generally as a physical problem such as heart or thyroid problems. This difference may have something to do with the way society views men and women. Throughout history, women have been unfairly considered more emotionally unstable than men, so experts may be more willing to consider an anxiety diagnosis for women. Furthermore, women are more likely to develop anxiety due to sexist treatment. For men, it is considered inappropriate to express sadness or fear, as these are considered signs of weakness. Men are more likely to express anger to cover up their fear. These attitudes toward both women and men are outdated, but they are unfortunately often reinforced to this day, even when people are not consciously aware of it.

When it comes to seeking help for an anxiety disorder, gender as well as race have an effect. Men, on the whole, are less likely to seek medical or psychological help when they have problems that affect their physical or mental health. They are also more likely to deny to others—and even to themselves—that they have a problem at all. This may be because, regardless of culture or race, most men do not want to appear weak in any way. They associate anxiety disorders with emotional problems, and emotional issues are often considered women's problems. Some men who suffer from panic disorder turn to alcohol or drug abuse to dull the symptoms. In a study of men and women with agoraphobia, which often accompanies panic disorder, nearly twice as many men as women were alcoholics. This can jeopardize and eventually destroy careers, friendships, and families.

A 2019 study by the U.S. Department of Health and Human Services found that the people who were most likely to seek and receive mental health treatment were white adults, young adults, women, people in higher income brackets, and people who live in cities. The study found that the high expense of services and participants' lack of insurance were the most common reasons why someone would not seek help. Addressing these problems will require a drastic change in society.

MYTH: "YOU COULD CONTROL YOUR ANXIETY IF YOU TRIED"

When a loved one suffers from an anxiety disorder, family members and friends face a variety of challenges that can lead to frustration. One problem is isolation. Often, the person suffering from the anxiety disorder becomes socially isolated; however, this isolation can carry over into the family as well.

For instance, a mother may have panic attacks, which means her child may not be allowed to invite friends over to the house. Parents with SAD may not be able to attend their children's recitals, plays,

SAME DISORDER, DIFFERENT REACTIONS

One thing that people—even people who have an anxiety disorder—may not understand is that anxiety disorders affect people in different ways. These differences seem obvious when comparing the different disorders, but even within the same disorder, reactions can vary from person to person. One person with panic disorder may hide their panic attacks very well, while another person's panic attacks may be very obvious. This can unfortunately lead to people accusing others of lying about having a disorder, especially if the symptoms are not obvious to anyone except the sufferer's close friends and family. It is important for everyone to remember that people react in different ways to their anxiety, and those reactions often depend on things such as how strong the anxious feelings are, whether a person feels as if they are in a safe place, and whether someone trusts the people around them. No one should ever tell someone that their anxiety is not legitimate simply because they are not reacting the way someone else thought they would.

An anxiety disorder affects the person who has it as well as the people around them. The extra stress this places on relationships can be upsetting for all involved.

or sporting events, which can be frustrating for the child. Neighbors may ask questions about why a certain family member is never seen outside the house, which can be uncomfortable for the rest of the family to discuss. Additionally, anxiety often causes irritability and poor concentration, which can lead to arguments between family members. If the person with anxiety turns to alcohol or drugs as a way to cope, it can further disrupt their family members' lives.

When a child has an anxiety disorder, some parents might first think it is a phase—just some part of childhood that their child will outgrow. In the beginning, they may ignore or rationalize the outward symptoms of the disorder. Some parents believe their child is acting out for attention, and they mistakenly believe the best way to deal with that is to withhold that attention. Other parents feel guilty, wondering if they are doing something to cause the child's problem. These parents may go along with the behavior, treating it as normal and acceptable. By adapting the home environment to the disorder, trying to make things "easier" for the child, and even expecting siblings to go along with the behavior, the parents make themselves part of the problem, rather than seeking help and working toward a solution. Over time, if the behaviors continue, family members may become angry or impatient. They may think the child should just snap out of it, but people do not snap out of anxiety disorders. As with any other health problem, children and adults with anxiety disorders generally do not recover or improve without the proper treatment.

Some people still attach a stigma to anxiety disorders and may say things such as, "It's all in your head," "Just try not to worry so much," or even, "You could control it if you tried." They may suggest solutions the person has already tried and accuse them of not trying hard enough if the person says those solutions have not worked. It is important for people who do not have an anxiety disorder to remember that people who do have a disorder often try very hard to control it. Just as no one would tell someone with cancer to simply try harder not to be sick, no one should tell a person with a mental illness that they would get better if they just tried harder. A person with an anxiety disorder does not choose to have the disorder, and having it does not make them a bad or weak person.

As awareness of anxiety disorders grows, more people are beginning to understand and accept that anxiety is a mental illness that is difficult for someone to control on their own. However, panic or anxiety attacks can be stressful and sometimes scary to watch, and someone may not always know the right way to react the first few times they see it happening. Some ways to support a friend or family member with anxiety include:

- listening to and acknowledging what they are saying
- staying calm
- letting them know you are there for them and care about them
- asking them how you can help

- asking before you touch them
- learning how to recognize signs that they are anxious
- learning how to calm them down

Everyone reacts differently to their own anxiety, so what works for one person may not work for another. Some may find hugs to be calming, while others may not want to be touched. Some may find that being asked questions helps them pull themselves out of a mental spiral, while for others, being the center of attention may make them panic more. It is important to ask the person what they want instead of assuming, and it is just as important for the person dealing with anxiety to communicate their needs when asked. Having a

Some people find hugs calming when they are having a panic attack. Others get more panicked when they are touched, even by a loved one. Always ask before touching someone who is having a panic attack.

conversation about this while everyone is calm can be useful. After the anxiety passes, the person often feels guilty or ashamed because they know their emotions were out of proportion to the actual situation, so they may need reassurance that they did not do anything wrong and that their friends and family still love and accept them.

MYTH: "ANXIETY ISN'T A SERIOUS PROBLEM"

Many people feel that humor helps them handle their mental illness better. However, when the jokes are made by someone who does not experience a disorder on a daily basis, they can be very offensive and even harmful. One unfortunately common thing people with an anxiety disorder must deal with is people believing that their condition is not real or serious because people use terms associated with anxiety disorders so often to jokingly refer to normal behaviors. Rachel Griffin, a contributor to the *Huffington Post*, wrote:

> *Mental health conditions aren't words you can just throw around to describe people. Your ex isn't* so bipolar *because your relationship was up and down … Your brother isn't* so OCD *because he's a fastidious [person] and likes to match his sneakers to his outfit. The politician [whose] ideas you don't like isn't* psychotic. *Many people who have mental health conditions are people you would never suspect have them … Stop calling people acting in negative ways* mentally ill. *It's incredibly offensive to people with mental health conditions.*[10]

Some companies have been criticized for creating products that make light of mental illness. For instance, in 2015, Target came under fire for selling a shirt that said, "OCD: Obsessive Christmas Disorder."

This spreads the idea that OCD is a harmless quirk rather than a severe mental illness that disrupts the lives of people who suffer from it.

Urban Outfitters also received harsh criticism for selling shirts that mocked or made light of substance abuse ("Misery Loves Alcohol") and anorexia ("Eat Less"). The company also marketed flasks for alcohol that were shaped like prescription drug bottles, reinforcing the idea that alcohol is a legitimate form of medication, when in fact it does not solve problems; it only causes them. Products such as these contribute to the stigma surrounding mental illness, treating it as a joke and subtly encouraging people to deal with it on their own in unhealthy ways, rather than seeking help from a professional.

Because all people deal with feelings of anxiety from time to time, some have trouble understanding that an anxiety disorder is not the same as typical feelings of worry or stress. However, anxiety disorders are real health problems that deserve to be taken seriously.

TREATMENTS

It is important to understand and challenge misconceptions about anxiety disorders because those misconceptions can be barriers to treatment. A person will not seek treatment unless they know something is wrong, but even when they feel that their responses to situations are not normal, they often let themselves be convinced by the labels others place on them. Someone with an anxiety disorder may be described as "a worrywart," "high-strung," "shy," "antisocial," or "uptight." They may be told they need to face their fears in order to get over them or that they need to stop worrying altogether. When they eventually get a diagnosis from a professional, it may come as a relief to them to know that although their fears are, indeed, all in their head, it is not their fault that they cannot just "get over it."

When someone does receive a diagnosis, they can begin treatment. Some people may be able to overcome their disorder with therapy alone, while others may need medication on either a short-term or long-term basis. Just as there is a stigma attached to seeking therapy, there is a stigma attached to taking medication. Some people may feel that taking medication is a sign of weakness and refer to it as a "crutch," or something that keeps someone from truly getting over their disorder. However, just as awareness of the symptoms of anxiety disorders has been growing, awareness of some people's genuine need for medication to control these symptoms has also been growing. Kristen Bell has spoken out against the stigma, saying, "If you do decide to go on a prescription to help yourself, understand that the world wants to shame you for that, but in the medical community, you would never deny a diabetic his insulin."[11] Each individual must speak with their own doctors to evaluate the treatment path that is right for them.

GETTING A DIAGNOSIS

As with any type of illness, the first steps toward recovery are seeking help and being diagnosed correctly by a doctor. This process can be quite tricky because anxiety is a symptom of so many different disorders, including schizophrenia, a mental disorder characterized by delusions and hallucinations. Anxiety can also result from physical conditions, such as diseases of the brain, some types of heart disease, and hyperglycemia, which is an abnormally high amount of sugar in the blood, often associated with diabetes.

Some medical conditions can cause anxiety.

Even the patient's diet needs to be evaluated for foods and drinks high in caffeine, which can also produce symptoms of anxiety.

Since anxiety can be caused by so many different conditions, doctors should be thorough in their evaluations. They need to know the patient's medical history, a general medical history of close family members to determine if any anxiety-related conditions run in the family, and a complete list of medications the patient is currently taking. Additionally, the patient—and sometimes the patient's family—will sometimes be interviewed by psychiatric specialists. This part of the diagnostic process generally consists of interviews, several short-answer questionnaires, and symptom lists. One commonly used tool is the Anxiety Disorders Interview Schedule (ADIS).

The ADIS is a structured interview to determine a patient's current feelings of anxiety and to diagnose which anxiety disorder or disorders the patient is presently experiencing, according to the criteria listed in the *DSM*. Additionally, it contains a section on family

Talking to someone about anxiety can be very helpful. A therapist is best because they can teach coping skills, but a loved one can offer support and sympathy.

psychiatric history and helps determine whether or not the anxiety problem is tied to substance abuse. There are both an adult version and a two-part, parent-and-child version for younger patients.

In addition to psychological evaluations, the patient may also be tested to determine if the anxiety problems are linked to any physical conditions, such as low blood sugar or thyroid problems. However, these conditions have other symptoms as well, so if the patient's only symptom is anxiety, the doctor may not run any tests at all aside from a routine checkup.

As with the diagnostic process for any disease or condition, these steps take time. There is no such thing as an instant diagnosis. Doctors need to gather and evaluate all the data to have the relevant facts at hand to make the best diagnosis for the patient. The medical team will then work with the patient to determine the best course of treatment, which generally consists of therapy, either alone or with medication.

WHICH IS WHICH?

It can sometimes be confusing for people to distinguish between a therapist, psychologist, and psychiatrist. "Therapist" is a more general term used to refer to anyone, including social workers, marriage counselors, and psychologists, who helps patients learn how to deal with their emotional and mental problems.

Psychologists have a degree in psychology and are able to diagnose mental disorders through psychological testing. They provide therapy as treatment for mental illnesses, but they are not qualified to prescribe medications. If they determine that a patient needs a certain type of medication as a way to treat their mental illness, they will refer them to a psychiatrist, who is a medical doctor who has a degree in psychiatry. In other words, a psychologist will generally focus on ways to change behavior and thoughts, while a psychiatrist more commonly evaluates medications a patient is taking and whether or not they are working effectively to treat their mental illness.

HEALTHY COPING MECHANISMS

Therapy is an approach to treating mental disorders that can be used alone or with medication. A large part of therapy involves verbal communication. The appropriate type of therapy chosen for the patient is supervised by therapists with special training in specific areas. Therapy's effectiveness as a treatment tool is described by Dr. John March, a professor of psychology and psychiatry at Duke Clinical Research Institute in Durham, North Carolina:

> *Medication … is effective to get an immediate reduction of symptoms. However, its effects only last as long as the patient takes the drug. Research shows that combination therapies or CBT [cognitive behavioral therapy] alone have longer lasting effects and help prevent relapse.*[12]

Therapy is not one type of treatment, but many. These include art therapy, CBT, and exposure therapy, among others. A prescribed course of therapy can be short term, requiring just a few visits with a qualified therapist. More likely, though, it will continue for a longer period of time, even up to a number of years. Therapy sessions might involve one person, couples, or even entire families, depending on the patient's need.

Art therapy helps people who have difficulty expressing themselves in words. In addition to drawing or painting, art therapy includes drama, music, poetry, and dance. This type of therapy can help people cope with certain traumatic experiences. This is especially true of children who have been traumatized by family violence. Younger children may not have sufficient vocabulary to express their feelings, but they can draw them or act them out. This not only helps the child express their feelings, but also gives therapists a clearer picture of the types of trauma the child has experienced.

Creating art can help with anxiety.

CBT helps the patient change unwanted, unhealthy, or inappropriate thoughts and behaviors. It is talk therapy based on the theory that people can change their feelings if they can change their thoughts. For instance, if a person's anxiety causes them to think things such as, "I'm annoying and no one likes me," a therapist can help them change that thought to something positive, such as, "I have a lot of friends who love me." Over time, as the person starts believing the positive thought, their anxiety over that particular issue will typically decrease.

In exposure therapy, the patient is repeatedly but safely exposed to the place, object, person, or situation that causes the anxiety. According to experts who use this type of therapy in treating their patients, exposure to the objects or events that cause the anxious thoughts will, over time, make the unwanted thoughts stop occurring.

Another type of therapy is called eye movement desensitization and reprocessing (EMDR) therapy. In this type of therapy, the patient "will pay attention to a back-and-forth movement or sound while [thinking] about [an] upsetting memory long enough for it to become less distressing."[13] This type of therapy is somewhat controversial because although studies show that it is effective at treating PTSD, most also show that it is no more effective than standard exposure therapy. Therefore, many people believe the eye movements are unnecessary. At the same time, there is no evidence that the movements are harmful, so some people continue to use EMDR as long as their patient is seeing results.

USING MEDICATION

Once the diagnostic process is complete, a doctor may determine that the patient could benefit from taking medication from the groups of drugs that have been developed for use in the treatment of mental disorders. Medication is generally prescribed if the anxiety symptoms are serious to the point that they interfere with the patient's daily life. These drug groups include selective serotonin reuptake inhibitors (SSRIs), beta-blockers, and benzodiazepines. These drug groups act in the body in different ways to treat symptoms of anxiety disorders.

For quite some time, the group most commonly prescribed for symptoms of anxiety disorders was benzodiazepines. Now, though, doctors limit the use of this group of drugs to the most severe cases of anxiety to limit the potential for addiction. Benzodiazepines work by increasing the effectiveness of a neurotransmitter called gamma-aminobutyric acid (GABA), which calms the brain. This group of drugs can be given orally, or in extreme cases when the patient needs to be sedated, they can be

Some medications interact with each other or with certain foods. For example, grapefruit can make some anxiety medications less effective. Checking labels is important.

injected. Diazepam (Valium), alprazolam (Xanax), clonazepam (Klonopin), and lorazepam (Ativan) are the most commonly prescribed benzodiazepines. Each drug has benefits and drawbacks and can be used in different situations. As with other drug groups, benzodiazepines have side effects. For example, if the patient takes them longer than a few weeks or takes more pills at one time than recommended, they can become both physically and psychologically addicted to the drugs. Their body can become used to, or tolerant of, the drugs, and this means that to produce the same results, the patient will need stronger and stronger doses. When someone has developed an addiction to any drug, either prescribed or illegal, the person has to go through an uncomfortable and difficult time called withdrawal to break free of the drug. Symptoms of benzodiazepine withdrawal syndrome include confusion, loss of appetite, shaking, sweating, insomnia, and ringing in the ears. Additionally, taking them with alcohol can be life-threatening.

Because benzodiazepines are generally only given for short-term use, doctors may choose to prescribe an antidepressant in addition to or instead of a benzodiazepine, with the benzodiazepine being used only to calm the most severe panic attacks. Antidepressants can be given to patients over a longer period of time with less chance of the patients building a tolerance and becoming addicted.

SSRIs are the most commonly prescribed type of antidepressant. They work by preventing a neurotransmitter, or chemical messenger in the brain, called serotonin from getting reabsorbed by nerve cells after it is released. This is beneficial because "keeping levels of the neurotransmitters higher could improve communication between the nerve cells—and that can strengthen circuits in the brain which regulate mood."[14] SSRIs include sertraline (Zoloft), paroxetine (Paxil), escitalopram (Lexapro), and fluoxetine (Prozac). Side effects of these drugs include drowsiness, nausea, insomnia, and headaches. In some cases, they can increase rather than decrease anxiety and depression.

People who experience anxiety as a result of PMDD may be prescribed an SSRI to take only during the two weeks before their period, when their

PMDD symptoms are present. Although antidepressants typically have to build up in a person's system to have an effect, *Harvard Health Publications* wrote that SSRIs "alleviate PMDD more quickly than depression, which means that women don't necessarily have to take the drugs every day."[15] However, this type of treatment is risky, as cycling on and off the medication can increase the risk of side effects such as stomach problems and suicidal thoughts.

Another group of drugs sometimes used to treat anxiety disorders is beta-blockers. This type of medication is often used to treat high blood pressure, but it is sometimes also prescribed for anxiety because it blocks the effects of epinephrine, or adrenaline. This means a person does not feel the physical effects of anxiety, such as increased heart rate, sweating, and trembling. However, beta-blockers do nothing to treat anxious thoughts, so they are not helpful for everyone. However, according to *University Health News*, "when you face your fear, whatever it is, without having the physical symptoms you normally associate with fear, eventually that fear often diminishes or even goes away [altogether]. Because of this, beta blockers can be beneficial in combination with cognitive behavior therapy … in order to help people overcome specific fears and phobias."[16] Beta-blockers are less useful for people with GAD because in the case of that disorder, anxiety is typically not triggered by one particular thing. Side effects of beta-blockers may include fatigue, weight gain, dizziness, and cold hands.

Some drug groups that were commonly used in the past have become outdated thanks to scientific advancements. These include tricyclic antidepressants (TCAs) and monoamine oxidase inhibitors (MAOIs). Named for the three rings of atoms in their molecular structure, TCAs have been around since the 1950s. They work by helping two neurotransmitters, norepinepherine and serotonin, work effectively in the brain. TCAs help keep these chemical messengers active by preventing them from being reabsorbed. Among several of these antidepressants are amitriptyline (Elavil) and amoxapine (Moxadil).

MAOIs are no longer commonly prescribed. One of the dangers of this class of medication is that they have serious interactions with many different common foods, such as cheese.

When SSRIs were created in the late 1980s, they generally replaced TCAs because SSRIs have milder side effects. Today, TCAs are often a last resort, given only when other medications do not work.

MAOIs prevent monoamine oxidase, a liver and brain enzyme, from doing its clean-up job. Monoamine oxidase burns up the neurotransmitters serotonin, norepinephrine, and dopamine once they have done their part in transmitting messages to the brain. If monoamine oxidase is prevented from doing its job, the neurotransmitters begin to build up. This can lower anxiety and ease depression in some patients.

MAOIs are almost never prescribed anymore due to the side effects that can occur, especially when patients eat certain foods. These side effects include dizziness, drowsiness, and blurred vision. Patients cannot eat cheeses, pickled foods, or chocolates, and they cannot drink alcoholic or nonalcoholic beers or wines when taking MAOIs because a substance called tryamine will flood the brain. When MAOIs keep monoamine oxidase from doing its job, one of the other substances it cannot mop up is tryamine. This substance causes blood pressure to rise. Excessive amounts of tryamine can cause blood pressure to rise so severely that blood vessels burst in the brain.

Many antidepressant and antianxiety medications are not suitable for people under the age of 18 because they are too powerful for bodies that are still growing and developing. Some exceptions are Prozac, Zoloft, and clomipramine (Anafranil), which are antidepressants approved by the U.S. Food and Drug Administration (FDA) to treat certain disorders, such as OCD, in children and teens.

It is important for someone taking an antidepressant to remember that, although these drugs are generally considered safe, stopping a drug after taking it for a long time can result in withdrawal symptoms. Patients must be weaned off the drug by taking smaller and smaller doses over a period of time.

Different drugs affect people differently. What works for one person may not work for another. For this reason, no one should ever, under any circumstances, take a drug that has been prescribed to a friend or relative, as the results can be unpredictable and dangerous. Additionally, someone who has been prescribed a drug should discuss the side effects and possible interactions with their doctor and pharmacist. Finding the right medication can be a long process for those dealing with mental disorders. Many people have to try more than one drug to find the one that works best for them. However, when they find the right one, the results are worth the wait.

DO YOUR RESEARCH

People living with an anxiety disorder may sometimes feel that they will do anything to make their anxiety go away quickly, and unfortunately, sometimes unethical people take advantage of this fact in order to make money. They may sell products that are not proven to work, such as pills or self-help books, at very high prices. Additionally, some people who suffer from anxiety disorders may swear by one particular treatment that helped them personally, but this does not mean it will help everyone, even people with the same disorder. The ADAA offers some advice to keep in mind:

- *Look for credentials. Look for academic degrees, professional and state licenses, association memberships, and other evidence of experience for the authors of any website. A "leading expert" or fellow panic sufferer might not offer the treatment that's best for you …*
- *Beware of extravagant claims—instant cures, guaranteed results of never again having anxiety symptoms, revolutionary formulas, "natural" or unique methods or techniques that require payment—and products "exclusively available from this website." Just because it says "scientifically proven" doesn't mean it's true.*
- *When you participate in a forum, message board, or chat room, be aware that while it's easy to get information from other people that appears helpful, it may work against your recovery. Peers may offer valuable insight, but be sure to check any advice with a mental health professional.*[1]

1. "Myth-Conceptions, About Anxiety," Anxiety and Depression Association of America. www.adaa.org/understanding-anxiety/myth-conceptions.

When someone finds the particular drug that works for them and begins to feel relief from anxiety, it is common for them to start to believe that they have been "cured" and no longer need to take the drug. Unfortunately, they often find that their symptoms return when the medication is out of their system.

Anxiety can cause tense muscles. When the body learns this connection, tenseness for other reasons can also trigger anxiety. Getting a massage can help with both the physical and mental effects of anxiety.

Some people only need medications for a short while and do find that they feel better even after stopping them, but this situation should be discussed with their doctors beforehand, especially if they are taking a drug that requires tapering off to avoid withdrawal.

CHANGES IN LIFESTYLE

The path to recovery for patients is not limited to therapy and medications. In some instances, alternative therapies have proven successful in relieving anxiety. Some people use these forms of therapy along with more conventional therapies, while others try to rely on alternative therapies alone. These alternative therapies include massage, aromatherapy, vitamin supplements, and diet changes.

Massage therapy has been shown to lower anxiety and stress and decrease the hormones that cause stress.

In a study conducted at the Touch Research Institute at the University of Miami School of Medicine, one group of subjects was given a chair massage twice a week for five weeks. The control group—the group of people who did not receive a massage—was directed to simply relax in the massage chairs for 15 minutes. Both groups were monitored by means of an electroencephalogram (EEG) before, during, and immediately after the study period. An EEG measures changes in the brain, so researchers could see how people's brain activity changed in response to either getting or not getting a massage. The participants were rated on several psychological scales before and after the study period. In addition to clearly lowered anxiety levels, the group receiving the massage showed enhanced alertness and increased speed and accuracy in math skills over the control group. This study indicates that massage therapy benefits people not only by relieving anxiety, but also by improving mental alertness.

Aromatherapy also appears to benefit some people by lowering anxiety. According to aromatherapists, using certain fragrant substances in lotions and sprays can improve mood and overall general health. Some scents, such as lavender and sandalwood, seem to have a calming effect on people. Aromatherapists believe that the use of these products can enhance the beneficial effects of other types of treatment by helping the patient relax.

A number of studies have determined that anxiety can also be relieved by making adjustments in diet. According to research, caffeine, salt, preservatives, hormones in meat, and refined sugar can elevate anxiety. People may be able to reduce their anxiety by avoiding foods that contain these ingredients. Avoiding coffee and alcohol can also help. These substances can interrupt sleep and increase anxiety.

Although teas that contain caffeine can increase anxiety, chamomile tea has been shown to reduce anxiety. Studies show that it can make people feel more sleepy and relaxed, possibly because of a substance in the tea that binds to benzodiazepine receptors in the brain. However, since chamomile is an herb, these substances are present in much lower amounts than they would be in a medication. For this reason, the effects are not as powerful as they are with a pharmaceutical drug. Chamomile tea may be sufficient for mild anxiety, or it may help reduce anxiety in combination with prescription drugs.

Mindfulness activities, such as meditation and yoga, have also been shown to be helpful for anxiety. A person who is panicking will naturally take short, shallow breaths. If they are able to control their breathing and take longer, deeper breaths, this sends the message to the body that there is no danger, and the anxiety may disappear or lessen.

It is important to remember that, as with prescribed medications, alternative therapies vary in effectiveness from person to person. One person may have great success with aromatherapy and dietary changes, while another may experience no benefits at all. Some people believe alternative therapies only work because of the placebo effect, which describes a case where a person's mind tricks them into thinking the therapy is working. For example, someone may believe aromatherapy is helping them, but they are actually calming down because they are taking deeper, slower breaths to smell the pleasant scent. For this reason, it can be good to safely experiment with different therapies to see how helpful they really are.

Some people have strong opinions on whether or not pharmaceutical drugs are helpful. Many people believe that natural is better, although this is not always the case; some synthetic, or man-made,

Taking care of the body can have amazing impacts on the mind. When people's bodies feel good, they often worry less. Eating a diet rich in nutrients and getting at least 30 minutes of movement each day are two ways to take care of physical and mental health at the same time.

medications are very helpful, just as some plants are poisonous. Additionally, dietary supplements are not regulated by the FDA, so the companies that make these products are not required to warn people about any possible side effects.

Some people choose not to take synthetic medications because they find that they feel worse on the medication than off it or that their symptoms are mild enough to be controlled with things such as diet and exercise. Others find that their quality of life improves immensely when they take medication. The decision to use or not use medication or alternative therapies is an extremely personal one that should be discussed with a doctor. Some people may share what has worked for them, but unless someone has asked for advice, this is not likely to be well received.

MOVEMENT AND ENDORPHINS

Movement is good for the body in a variety of ways. In addition to improving the function of the cardiovascular, muscular, and respiratory systems, movement is good for mental health. The brain and the body react chemically to movement, which contributes to an overall feeling of relaxation. In fact, when someone moves their body, the body generates the production of substances, such as serotonin and endorphins, that send calming messages to the brain. While serotonin sends chemical "feel good" messages to the brain, endorphins act as natural painkillers in the body. Together, these substances lower stress and anxiety and cause a feeling of well-being. Just 30 to 40 minutes of aerobic activity three or four times a week stimulates the body's production of these chemicals. The movement can be walking, jogging, bicycling, playing a sport, swimming, or another kind of physical activity.

Movement can reduce muscle tension, which is one effect of stress and anxiety. It is also a healthy outlet for the "fight or flight" state caused by anxiety. In addition to raising stress-lowering hormones, movement also reduces chemicals in the body that increase stress.

One type of movement that some people find especially helpful in relieving stress and anxiety is yoga.

Mindfulness is a good way to deal with anxiety symptoms.

Yoga is a combination of breathing exercises, postures, and meditation that are practiced in order to achieve connection with the body and the mind. With yoga, a person can learn breathing techniques that help achieve relaxation and a sense of calm. The yoga postures stretch the muscles, relieving tension and relaxing the body, and meditation calms and focuses the mind, which can also help relieve stress.

No single type of treatment is a "magic cure" that will totally rid a person of anxiety disorders. A combination of therapies may be more effective. Additionally, patients must realize that there are no quick fixes for anxiety disorders. Some people who have normal levels of stress and anxiety do not understand that someone with an anxiety disorder feels much worse and has a harder time controlling those feelings than they do. This can lead someone who has benefitted from yoga, dietary changes, or other management techniques to reduce their feelings of anxiety or stress to insist that people with an anxiety disorder do not need medication. They may even go so far as to shame people for taking it. However, many people with anxiety disorders see the most benefit when they combine their use of medication with sessions with a therapist and alternative treatments that work for them.

CHAPTER FOUR

COPING MECHANISMS

Unlike a physical illness, anxiety is not generally something that can be fully healed or cured. The goal of treatment is often to diminish the symptoms and help people learn how to function in everyday life. People with an anxiety disorder may still experience anxiety from time to time but will be better able to handle it on their own after successful treatment. According to JR Thorpe, a writer for the website Bustle:

> *It's helpful for people to comprehend mental health difficulties as, say, comparable to a broken leg when asking them to contemplate the real, physical obstacles of a serious brain issue. But there's a limit to the analogy, and that's the fact that mental health problems are* extremely *individual. Some may fade over time, others may go through phases of severity, and still others can be with the person for life. If they're going to be compared to anything physical, possibly mental health problems are most similar to a chronic pain condition, with highly individual details, a very unclear future, and a focus more on management than on "cures".*[17]

Some people may feel that treatment is useless if it will not result in a cure, but the truth is that people who undergo treatment are generally pleased with the progress they make in controlling the symptoms of their anxiety disorder. Thinking of treatment in terms of providing a cure can actually be harmful for people, as it creates the idea that if they still have anxiety, they have failed in some way. In reality, people who go through treatment are working very hard to get to a point where they have more good days than bad ones.

LEARNING HOW TO COPE

The challenges of daily life can cause stress and anxiety and can make an exisiting anxiety disorder more difficult to deal with. These stressors can range from widespread issues such as threats of terrorism, climate change, political actions, and the general safety and welfare of one's family members, to personal issues such as relationships, jobs, and money problems. Whatever the issue, there are a variety of methods people can use to cope with them. These methods may not work for everyone. This does not mean the person has failed; finding the right coping mechanism is a process of trial and error, and if people keep an open mind while trying things and do not immediately assume nothing will work, they will eventually be able to identify what does work for them.

One coping mechanism is a five-step exercise that involves monitoring thoughts and reactions. Step one is to identify the specific issue that is causing the stress. This might be a job interview, a final exam, an interaction with a specific person, or the death of a close friend or family member. The second step is to identify all personal thoughts related to the stressful situation. These thoughts may be realistic and based on facts, or irrational and based on fears. The next step is focusing on the negative thoughts and reactions. Physical responses might be a stiff neck, headache, upset stomach, or loss of sleep. Emotional reactions could be nervousness, severe depression, anger, or feelings of guilt. Behavioral reactions may include binge eating, avoiding people, or avoiding the issue that is causing the stress.

The fourth step involves confronting the negative responses and seeing them for what they are: self-defeating. This can be difficult, because these negative responses may have been influencing the person's life for so long that they have become habit. These may include self put-downs, over-generalizing thoughts such as, "Things are awful now and they'll stay that way forever," and all-or-nothing thinking, such as, "If I don't get a good grade on this test, I am an utter failure." Other negative responses are the tendency to jump to negative conclusions ("My friend hasn't responded to my text in over an hour. She must be mad at me."); mistaking feelings for facts ("My partner sat on the chair next to the couch instead of on the couch with me. He's rejecting me."); or converting positives into negatives ("Getting a good grade on this test will make it worse if I fail the next one.").

The final step is to replace the negative or inaccurate ideas with positive, accurate ones. This, too, can be difficult, because spontaneous negative thoughts are hard to control. Working with a therapist can give someone tools to do this and give them an opportunity to discuss things that did or did not work. Identifying what does not work allows people to change their treatment plans until they find something that does work.

Despite their best efforts, people do backslide once in a while. It is important to remember that these things do not make someone a bad or worthless person or a failure. It is also important to focus on successes, even the small ones. Going all day without obsessing about fears is a major achievement, and people should congratulate themselves for it. Some situations are harder than others to put these efforts into practice, but these steps are like taking piano lessons: Skills improve with practice.

A person coping with one or more anxiety disorders should set goals, but these goals should be realistic.

For instance, a person with SAD cannot suddenly decide to give a speech in class when they have been struggling to talk to even their closest friends. The person might begin by spending an hour with a friend in a social setting such as a coffeeshop. This is a realistic goal, and goals like it can be expanded over time. Starting with an all-or-nothing approach sets the person up for failure, which reinforces their negative belief that they are incapable of overcoming their anxious behaviors.

One approach to coping with anxious feelings is to be proactive. For instance, someone who worries over the safety of family members can develop a disaster-readiness plan, which would include a list of food items and other supplies that would help the family be more safe and secure in the event of a hurricane or some other type of catastrophic weather. Developing a plan such as this is one way of taking positive action. Also, many families have a fire escape plan, which includes a meeting place outside the home where everyone should gather in the event of a fire or a neighbor who would serve as a contact person if family members became separated. Taking action and having a plan often makes people feel more in control of their lives and more secure.

Another way to ease periods of anxiety is through meditation and visualization. Visualization is a way to temporarily send the mind to a "happy place." This happy place can be anywhere that the person considers relaxing and calm. The idea is to visualize the place and imagine actually being there. This place can be a cabin in the mountains, a quiet beach, or even a favorite park. This technique takes time and effort, but with practice, it may be possible to change a state of anxiety to a calm state.

However, this does not work for everyone. Some people find that it makes them more anxious because they have nothing to distract them, so their anxious thoughts become even more overwhelming. For these people, cleaning the house, listening to a podcast or audiobook, or watching their favorite TV show may be a better way to handle their anxiety.

Being in nature can be very calming. For people who live in a city, it can be helpful just to be in a room with plants.

Other strategies for coping on a daily basis include remembering that, although symptoms of anxiety issues such as panic and obsessive thoughts are frightening, they are neither dangerous nor harmful, and feelings of anxiety are just the mind and body's exaggerated reaction to something stressful. People's natural instinct is often to fight fear, especially when they are aware that it is out of proportion to what is happening. They may also try to act natural so no one will realize that they are upset. This can cause them to feel anxiety about their anxiety and then feel even more anxious when they are unable to force themselves to calm down. Some people find that when they do not fight the feelings of anxiety, those feelings actually decrease. Repeating a mantra, such as "I feel anxious right now and that's OK," may help someone deal with a panic attack.

SUCCESSFUL SUPPORT

People with anxiety disorders need the support of friends and family, but sometimes that support can

UNHELPFUL PHRASES

Sometimes people try to be supportive of a loved one with an anxiety disorder, but what they think of as comforting words may actually be frustrating or upsetting to the person with the disorder. Other times, people simply do not understand what someone with an anxiety disorder is going through, especially if the person's symptoms are not visible—for instance, someone who is feeling panic but hiding it well may be accused of lying about how scared they feel. Even other people with anxiety can sometimes say the wrong thing. Some things that are generally not helpful for someone with anxiety to hear include:

- "It's all in your head."
- "Calm down."
- "Just stop thinking about it."
- "I know how you feel; I get anxious too sometimes."
- "There's nothing to worry about."
- "You seem fine."
- "You're overreacting."
- "You would feel better if you [did yoga/meditated/ate healthier foods/etc.]."
- "Other people have much more severe anxiety than you do."
- "When I have a panic attack, I scream and cry. You look calm, so you can't possibly be having one right now/it must not be that bad."
- "Anxiety is just you holding yourself back from being happy."
- "Anxiety isn't a real mental illness."
- "If you tried harder, you could get over it."
- "There's nothing wrong in your life; other people have real problems to worry about."
- "You're too negative. Just think positive thoughts!"

cross a line into enabling. For example, if a family member has OCD, family and friends genuinely want to help their loved one. However, they need to understand that participating in rituals, such as repeatedly checking doors, windows, and appliances, or making sure that the person does not touch certain objects and become upset, does nothing to help that person cope with OCD. Helping the patient avoid a problem situation in the short term actually causes harm in the long term. Playing along enables the person to continue with the obsessive ritual or behavior. People often have the best of intentions when they enable their loved ones, believing that the condition will worsen if they do not engage in enabling behaviors.

To help break this cycle, a therapist works with their patient to help them understand that they should not try to get family members to manage their disorder for them, and sometimes with the patient's family members to encourage them to set boundaries so their own mental health does not suffer as well. The patient's family needs to understand that their loved one has to learn how to face difficult situations. Otherwise, the patient does not learn how to cope in a healthy way, while their loved ones suffer as a result of trying to manage someone else's mental illness for them.

Family and friends need to learn how to provide effective support. There is a middle ground between enabling someone and abandoning them. Family members need to educate themselves. They need to learn the types of anxiety disorders, their symptoms, and appropriate types of treatment. Family and friends must not be afraid to talk openly and without judgment about the condition with the person when that person is ready to discuss it. They need to understand that emotional highs and lows are to be expected as their loved one progresses toward recovery, and that feelings of frustration are normal. They can lend support by accompanying their loved one to therapy appointments, making sure the person knows that the disorder does not change the way family and friends feel about them, and, above all, being patient during what could be a lengthy treatment process.

Additionally, loved ones can celebrate the small successes. In this way, they are actively participating in a supportive way, acting as their loved one's cheering squad. They can help their loved one identify signs of backsliding into negative habits and remind them of steps to help manage these lapses. These types of encouragement help keep the negative, stressful feelings from returning. However, family members must not take on the role of therapist.

If the behavior of a person with an anxiety disorder has been affecting the whole family, they may benefit from attending therapy together.

As family members are showing support for their loved one, they may need to go into therapy themselves. Family therapy helps the family understand and cope with the patient's anxiety disorder. It promotes working together as a team rather than blaming each other, and it can prove helpful in revealing issues in the parents' or siblings' behavior that may be contributing, even unintentionally, to a person's anxiety disorder.

Family therapy can be useful in situations where the patient has been angrily lashing out at other family members. Even if everyone involved understands that it is the anxiety and frustration caused by the disorder that is responsible for the shouting in the first place, these verbal assaults can still result in hurt feelings all around. Family therapy can help repair this sort of emotional damage.

TAKING RESPONSIBILITY

Although anxiety disorders are mental illnesses whose effects on the brain and body cannot be controlled through sheer willpower, it is important to remember that having this disorder does not excuse poor behavior. It is not fair to anyone involved to dismiss hurtful words and actions by blaming the disorder. It makes friends and family feel upset and guilty, and it creates a sense of powerlessness for the person with the disorder. Feeling constantly out of control of their actions can increase the negative emotions that anxiety sufferers feel as a result of their illness, but knowing that they do have control over how they react to their illness can give them a sense of empowerment.

Many people feel that responsibility is the same thing as blame, but this is not true. People with any kind of anxiety disorder are not to blame for their feelings, but if their words or actions are hurtful to others, they should try to make amends. For instance, if someone has a panic attack, tries to leave a room quickly, and accidentally knocks over a lamp on the way out, they should later offer to pay for the lamp, even though they did not intend to break it. They do not need to feel guilty for breaking the lamp, but they should take responsibility for their action, even though it was an accident. Similarly, if their anxiety is making them feel irritable and they say something harsh to a loved one, they should apologize when they feel calmer. They should not tell the person, "I don't owe you an apology because my anxiety makes me irritable, and therefore, I can't be held accountable for anything I say."

Friends and family can help an anxiety sufferer and themselves by setting boundaries and being firm about sticking to those boundaries. For example, if someone with SAD asks their friend not to talk to anyone but them at a party, the friend may say, "That's not a reasonable thing to ask of me; I want to talk to other people and enjoy the party. However, I promise to come check on how you're doing every 20 minutes." It is important for friends and family to let an anxiety sufferer know that they will support them, but they will not regularly put their lives on hold. It is equally important for the anxiety sufferer to recognize when they are asking for something unreasonable and not to blame their support system for not caring enough or not doing enough. This is why therapy is an important tool: Managing emotions and taking personal responsibility is difficult and sometimes painful, and therapy can help people learn this skill.

Therapy is also helpful because it gives an anxiety sufferer someone to talk to besides friends and family. Although it is not unreasonable to expect loved ones to be sympathetic and listen to problems, the overwhelming nature of an anxiety disorder can sometimes be difficult for someone's loved ones to handle. It is possible for people with anxiety to unintentionally get so wrapped up in their own problems that they forget other people have problems as well. They may expect friends and family to constantly be available to listen at any hour of the day or night, try to one-up their friends with their own problems, or consistently change the subject of the conversation back to

PUTTING THOUGHTS IN WRITING

Some therapists ask their patients to keep journals as a part of their treatment, with the understanding that the patients have total control of the journals. The patients decide whether or not anyone else is allowed to read what is written in the journals. Since the patients have complete control of their journals, the therapists urge the patients to not hold back, to freely express feelings, and to be totally honest.

A good way to begin a journal is by setting aside time in the evening and writing about the day's activities, describing feelings and thoughts that accompanied the day's events. Some entries may be longer than others, but it is important to write daily. After a few weeks, it is often possible to look back through the entries and identify some of the actions, objects, or events that may be contributing to anxiety as well as personal actions that might be helpful in overcoming anxious feelings.

themselves. One aspect of taking personal responsibility for an illness is making an effort to show loved ones that they are appreciated. This can be as simple as allowing them time to talk about their own problems without judgment in a conversation. Good relationships—whether friendship, family, or romantic—are a two-way street, and both people must put in some effort to make it work.

SUPPORT GROUPS

In addition to individual and family therapy, support groups can be a lifeline for patients and families who are recovering from anxiety disorders or who are learning to cope while in the process of healing. Support groups are not therapy and are not intended to take the place of therapy. However, these groups can be helpful in addition to therapy. Even while undergoing treatment, people with anxiety disorders and their families can feel isolated. They sometimes feel as though there is no one else who could possibly understand how they feel. In support groups,

Joining a support group and meeting other people with similar struggles can help people with anxiety realize that they are not "broken" or "messed up."

patients and their families can get information about local resources. They can meet people with some of the same symptoms and discuss which types of coping skills have and have not been successful for other patients and their family members.

There are several ways to locate support groups. The professional in charge of a family member's treatment can refer both their patient and their family members to groups. Another way to find a patient or family support group is by contacting the mental health departments of local hospitals. Many hospitals have support group meetings onsite. Churches, synagogues, and other faith-based organizations may also have such referral information. A Google search for "support group," along with the particular anxiety disorder and the desired location—for instance, "phobia support groups in Chicago"—can also provide some possibilities.

Some people do not live in an area where local support groups are available. However, this does not mean they do not have access to the support organizations they need. A number of support groups are available online for people who have no such groups in their communities or for people who do not have access to transportation. Several things should be considered when choosing an online support group. For safety and security reasons, online support groups should require a login and a valid email address in order to join. For privacy, participants should be able to use screen names, and the site should be constantly moderated, preferably by mental health experts. If the patient has any concerns about a specific online group, it is best to ask their therapist or doctor. Therapists and doctors may be able to provide information about the online support groups best suited to their patients' needs and those sponsored by reputable organizations.

CHAPTER FIVE

MORE TO LEARN

Mental health experts have made a lot of strides in recent years toward identifying and treating anxiety disorders. However, there is always more to learn because even experts do not fully understand how the brain works. For instance, no one is completely sure what causes anxiety disorders; although chemical imbalances and environmental factors play a role, there is no way to predict who will develop an anxiety disorder. Some disorders may be genetic, which means they may be passed down from parent to child. However, there is no one specific gene for anxiety. According to Everyday Health, "For most people, genetic risk for anxiety is less likely to be an on/off switch than a complicated mix of genes that can put you at risk for developing anxiety. Even then your anxiety disorder might be different from your relative's in important ways."[18] It is still uncertain which is more responsible for the development of an anxiety disorder: a person's genes or learned behavior from living with a family member with anxiety. Researchers call this the "nature versus nurture" argument.

As researchers study anxiety disorders and their causes more closely, new and better treatments may be created. Since mental illnesses are highly individualized, it is unlikely that one cure-all pill or activity will ever be created, but over time, treatment methods may be refined so that they work even better than they currently do.

THE ROLE OF GENETICS

Gene therapy is a medical therapy in which altered genetic material is placed into living cells. Since there is evidence to show that anxiety disorders are at least partially genetic, gene therapy is being evaluated as a way to treat them. In gene therapy, genetic engineering is used to target certain genes in an effort to cure a disease. Genetic engineering is the science of developing and applying technologies that alter genetic material. By altering genetic material, unfavorable cellular traits that make a person more susceptible to physical and psychiatric illnesses can be modified, decreasing the chances of the person developing a serious mental or physical condition.

The idea that certain people carry genes that make them more likely to have certain psychiatric and medical conditions goes back many years, but London researcher Jonathan Flint and his colleagues at the Wellcome Trust Center for Human Genetics in Oxford, England, made significant progress in proving this idea, beginning in the early 1990s. They started tracking genetic effects in mice. They performed what is called an open field test, which is simply tracking a mouse's movements for five minutes in a brightly lit, unfamiliar environment, which for some mice is quite stressful. They discovered that, in stressful situations, mice behave much as humans do. The more anxious ones tended to hide and avoid the environment as much as they could. Then the scientists studied the genes of each generation of these mice, comparing the genes of those who appeared more anxious with the genes of those who behaved more calmly. They examined 84 genetic markers, finding 3 that appeared to account for the variations in behavior.

A genetic marker is a gene or DNA sequence that has an identified location on a chromosome and is associated with a certain trait. DNA is deoxyribonucleic acid, the material responsible for the genetic characteristics in all living things. These genetic markers can be detected in blood tests to determine if a person is at risk for developing a certain disease or condition.

In 2014, *Scientific American* reported on research done by Raül Andero Galí, a professor of behavioral sciences at Autonomous University of Barcelona. Galí and his team found a gene that is responsible for releasing a compound called brain-derived neurotrophic factor (BDNF), which has an effect on memories of fear. Galí believes this is important because mice that have a mutation in their BDNF gene prefer to be alone rather than spending time with other mice. Humans who have the same mutation report feeling fear for a longer than normal time after being startled.

Galí's research "has shown that a compound that mimics the effects of BDNF in the brain successfully helped mice get over fearful associations—specifically a sound paired with a foot shock. The prospect of BDNF gene therapy is also being investigated."[19] If this compound helps relieve fear in mice, the hope is that it will do the same for humans who suffer from anxiety disorders.

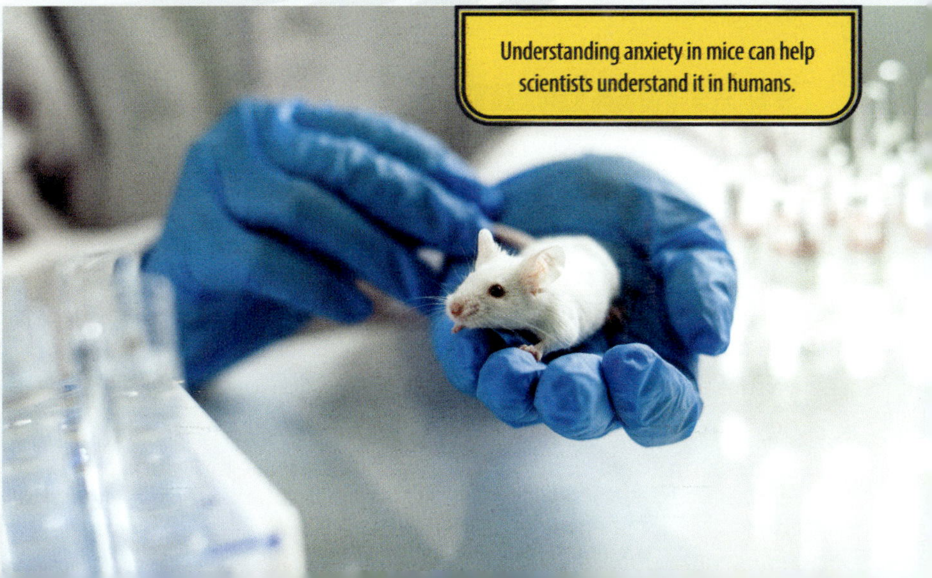

Understanding anxiety in mice can help scientists understand it in humans.

Although genes do play a role in anxiety, other studies have shown that the development of anxiety disorders also has a lot to do with environmental factors. In 2008, 909 pairs of twins, their children, and their spouses were studied in the Twin and Offspring Study in Sweden (TOSS). The study aimed to look at genetic and environmental influences on family relationships. In 2015, the data that related to anxiety was reexamined, and researchers found that there was almost no evidence that anxious parents passed their anxiety down to their children genetically. In other words, the study was "the first to clearly establish the early transmission of anxiety symptoms from parents to children, not through their shared genetic background, but rather from the way in which anxious parents raise their children. Parents who are anxious can now be counseled and educated on ways to minimize the impact of their anxiety on the child's development."[20]

Many researchers take the view that anxiety disorders develop as a result of a combination of genetic and environmental factors, but that combination may be different for everyone. A parent who has learned to control their anxiety may be able to help their children avoid developing the same disorder, but sometimes things outside their control still happen.

VR AS TREATMENT

One unexpected treatment option that is being explored for anxiety and other mental disorders is virtual reality (VR). VR is a computer-generated setting where people can participate and interact to a certain degree within an artificial or virtual environment. Since every element of the virtual environment can be controlled, this technology can be a useful tool in helping people overcome some symptoms of their anxiety disorders. It has the

GENERATIONAL TRAUMA

Although anxiety disorders may not be passed down through specific genes, researchers know that they can be passed down in families through behavior. A 2023 study followed 541 mother-child pairs over several years. The study started when the mothers were 26 weeks pregnant, and the mothers checked in with the researchers when their children were 3 months, 12 months, 24 months, 36 months, 4.5 years, and 6 years of age. When the children were between 7 and 8 years old, they filled out a survey to determine if they had anxiety or depression. The study found that mothers who had suffered trauma, including abuse or neglect, when they were children were more likely to have anxiety, depression, or both as adults. They were also more likely to have anxious or depressed children.

When trauma is passed down from parent to child this way, it is called "generational trauma." The Disney movie *Encanto* explored generational trauma, showing how the trauma Mirabel's grandmother had suffered as a young woman affected her behavior toward her children and grandchildren. The findings of the 2023 study and other past studies suggest that when one person in a family addresses their own mental health problems, everyone in the family benefits.

potential of being especially helpful in exposure therapy. In this type of VR therapy, patients are led through imaginary situations that bring on strong emotional responses, such as the fear and anxiety they experience when they are exposed to objects or events associated with their phobias. These experiences can include driving cars or being in high places. During the session, they are not allowed to use the avoidance strategies they often rely on in real situations. What makes VR especially effective is that, although it places patients in lifelike situations, the therapist is in total control of the virtual environment and can adjust the intensity of the emotionally threatening element. Nothing will happen that is not programmed by the therapist.

There are several benefits for the person receiving the treatment. The patient is spared the potential embarrassment of going through exposure therapy in public; the most anxiety-provoking aspects of situations such as crowded places, heights, and simulated takeoffs in aircraft can be replayed over and over to the point that these anxiety-causing issues become less threatening while never placing the patient in any physical danger; and the therapist can instantly end the virtual experience if it becomes too stressful for the patient. The patient experiences the anxiety of the event, but in the safety of a virtual environment.

VR is not standard practice for treating anxiety disorders at this time. There are a few different reasons for this. One is that VR equipment is still fairly expensive. Another is that many people see their therapist through online video calls, called

VR can be a way to safely put someone in high-stress situations so they can confront their fears.

"telehealth." Telehealth sessions became very common during the COVID-19 pandemic, when it was dangerous for people to be in close proximity to each other, and continued afterward because it is very convenient, especially for people with busy schedules who struggle to find time to drive to and from a therapist's office. A third reason is that not everyone can benefit from VR therapy, so not all therapists offer it. However, headsets have become much more widespread and easily obtainable in the past decade, which means the therapy is available to more people today. Many specialized VR therapy centers have opened up, and some individual therapists offer it as an option.

CLINICAL TRIALS

Many types of treatments and drugs for mental conditions as well as physical diseases are developed through a process called a clinical trial. A clinical trial is a scientific investigation of a drug, a device used in an invasive medical treatment, or a type of therapy, before it goes on the market or is used by the medical community.

Clinical trials are very important in developing new medications and treatments for all kinds of ailments, as well as finding new uses for existing substances. For example, lysergic acid diethylamide (LSD) is a hallucinogenic drug that has been taken recreationally—and illegally—for decades. A 2024 clinical trial found that one dose of a medication made with LSD provided relief from GAD for up to 12 weeks. It will still need to go through more trials before the FDA approves it, but the results are very promising. They show better treatment of anxiety symptoms than currently-available medications, with fewer side effects. Other illegal recreational drugs, such as MDMA (commonly known as ecstasy or molly) have been shown to do well treating other disorders, such as PTSD.

While clinical trials and other scientific studies are important, their quality can vary depending on the methods used to conduct them. It is important for people to be able to evaluate scientific studies so they can get a better sense of whether the results are accurate. Some questions for this kind of evaluation include:

1. *Was the study large enough to pass statistical muster?*
2. *Was it designed well?*
3. *Did it last long enough?*
4. *Were there any other possible explanations for the conclusions of the study or reasons to doubt the findings?*
5. *Do the conclusions fit with other scientific evidence? If not, why?*
6. *Do you have the full picture?*
7. *Have the findings been checked by other experts?*
8. *What are the implications of the research? Any potential problems or applications?*[21]

These things are important to consider because they have a strong impact on the results of a study. For instance, if a study is too small, it may not be representative of the general population. This means the study results might apply only to those few people and not be true for most people. If it lasted for only a short time, there might be long-term effects that no one knows about until after the drug has been approved, or the positive results might not last long. If the study has not been repeated by other scientists, it may be difficult to say whether the findings were the result of some kind of mistake or coincidence.

Additionally, it is important for people to be skeptical, or have a little bit of doubt, when they hear studies reported on the news, especially if those studies sound too good to be true. Scientific language can be difficult for the general public to understand, so many news shows simplify it when they report on studies. Sometimes they simplify it so much that it is no longer actually true. In 2016, *Last Week Tonight with John Oliver* aired a segment discussing some of the problems with reporting in scientific research. In one example, the Society for Maternal-Fetal Medicine published a study entitled "High-Flavanol Chocolate to Improve Placental Function and to Decrease the Risk of Preeclampsia: A Double Blind Randomized Clinical Trial." The study was trying to find out whether eating a small amount of chocolate would help pregnant women decrease their risk of preeclampsia, or high blood pressure during pregnancy. The study found that chocolate did not have a significant impact on the rate of preeclampsia, but the society issued a press release—a short summary of the study sent to news outlets—that simplified the language so it was easier to understand. The press release was entitled, "The Benefits of Chocolate During Pregnancy," so even though the study found that there were no real benefits, some news channels reported that chocolate could help pregnant women.

It is common for only positive study results to be reported, while the negative results are downplayed or ignored. Sometimes this is a result of a company only releasing the material that supports their product; other times, it is the result of a news show trying to put a good spin on something to attract more viewers. *Last Week Tonight with John Oliver* discussed a situation in which Fox News reported that a new study had found that driving dehydrated and driving drunk were equally dangerous. However, "as

Britain's National Health Service had already pointed out, that study was riddled with red flags, including that it was based on just 12 men—of whom data was only reported for 11—and it got funding from the European Hydration Institute, a foundation that has received over $7 million from Coca-Cola."[22] The fact that the money for the study came from a company that sells drinks should make people skeptical of the results, which encourage people to drink more.

Scientific research is important because it teaches people more about the world, and not every study is misleading. However, because so many studies are conducted every day, people should do their own research into the results to be more informed about treatments they are thinking of trying for anxiety.

HELPING PEOPLE UNDERSTAND

Two of the most important tools in battling any psy-

A LONG-TERM STUDY

The Netherlands Study of Depression and Anxiety (NESDA) is an ongoing long-term study that aims "to determine the (psychological, social, biological and genetic) factors that influence the development and the long-term prognosis of anxiety and depression."[1] The study began in 2004 with 2,981 participants and lasted for 15 years.

Through interviews, blood samples, medical records, and tests such as functional magnetic resonance imaging (fMRI), the researchers collected data with the goal of using it to eventually diagnose and treat anxiety and depression. Participants were asked questions about their alcohol and drug use, optimism, social support system, work environment, income, and many more topics to help researchers get the best overall picture of what contributes to the development of these disorders. After the study ended, other researchers were able to use the data in their own studies.

1. "About NESDA," Netherlands Study of Depression and Anxiety. www.nesda.nl/nesda-english/.

chiatric condition, including anxiety disorders, are knowledge and communication. Trying to ignore their very real presence in society or avoiding talking about them does not make them go away. Educational programs, communication, and support networks play an important role in understanding complex conditions of the mind.

The more people talk about GAD, SAD, panic disorder, separation anxiety, selective mutism, and phobias, the more these conditions will become normalized. People will get used to hearing about them and will understand that they exist and have very real consequences for the people who have to deal with them. This will help people be better equipped to assist friends, family, and even strangers who have an anxiety disorder. Discussing the symptoms, thoughts, and feelings associated with these illnesses can help mental health professionals make a unique treatment plan for each individual that will give better results than one generic treatment.

As medical and scientific knowledge continue to evolve, the ways in which anxiety disorders are diagnosed and treated will improve as well. Anxiety disorders may always be a risk for people, but as technology and medicine continue to advance, there is a real possibility that in the future, they will be managed better than has ever been possible before.

NOTES

INTRODUCTION: A STRESSFUL DISORDER

1. "Anxiety Disorders," National Institute of Mental Health, March 2016. www.nimh.nih.gov/health/topics/anxiety-disorders/index.shtml.
2. Quoted in Natasha Tracy, "Famous People Who Have Experienced an Anxiety Disorder," HealthyPlace.com, August 2, 2016. www.healthyplace.com/anxiety-panic/articles/famous-people-who-have-experienced-an-anxiety-disorder/.

CHAPTER ONE: WHAT IS ANXIETY?

3. Quoted in "Generalized Anxiety," BrainPhysics. www.brainphysics.com/generalized-anxiety.php.
4. "Panic Disorder & Agoraphobia," Anxiety and Depression Association of America. www.adaa.org/understanding-anxiety/panic-disorder-agoraphobia.
5. Quoted in "Panic Attacks," BrainPhysics. www.brainphysics.com/panic-attacks.php.
6. Quoted in Fred Penzel, *Obsessive-Compulsive Disorder: A Complete Guide to Getting Well and Staying Well.* New York, NY: Oxford University Press, 2000, p. 157.
7. Fred Penzel, "How Do I Know I'm Not Really Gay?," International OCD Foundation. iocdf.org/expert-opinions/homosexual-obsessions/.

CHAPTER TWO: MYTHS AND FACTS

8. "Facts," Anxiety and Depression Association of America. www.adaa.org/living-with-anxiety/women/facts.

9. "Women Are Diagnosed with PTSD More than Men, Even Though They Encounter Fewer Traumatic Events, Says Research," American Psychological Association, November 19, 2006. www.apa.org/news/press/releases/2006/11/ptsd-rates.aspx.

10. Rachel Griffin, "4 Jokes About Mental Illness You Need to Stop Making," *Huffington Post*, last modified January 11, 2017. www.huffingtonpost.com/rachel-griffin/4-jokes-about-mental-illness-you-need-to-stop-making_b_8932500.html.

CHAPTER THREE: TREATMENTS

11. Quoted in Sierra Marquina, "Kristen Bell Opens Up About Struggle with Anxiety and Depression: 'The World Wants to Shame You,'" *Us Weekly*, May 6, 2016. www.usmagazine.com/celebrity-news/news/kristen-bell-reveals-she-takes-prescription-for-anxiety-and-depression-w205585.

12. Quoted in Stephanie Sampson, "Anxiety in the Age of Innocence: Children and Anxiety Disorders," Anxiety Disorders Association of America. www.adaa.org/gettinghelp/newsletter/childrenAnxiety.asp.

13. "Eye Movement Desensitization and Reprocessing (EMDR) for PTSD," U.S. Department of Veterans Affairs, August 19, 2016. www.ptsd.va.gov/public/treatment/therapy-med/emdr-for-ptsd.asp.

14. Joseph Goldberg, "How Different Antidepressants Work," WebMD, August 15, 2015. www.webmd.com/depression/how-different-antidepressants-work#3.

15. "Treating Premenstrual Dysphoric Disorder," *Harvard Health Publications*, October 2009. www.health.harvard.edu/womens-health/treating-premenstrual-dysphoric-disorder.

16. Alison Palkhivala, "Stressed? Take Heart ... Beta Blockers for Anxiety Can Be Effective," *University Health News*, December 29, 2016. universityhealthnews.com/daily/stress-anxiety/beta-blockers-for-anxiety/.

CHAPTER FOUR: COPING MECHANISMS

17. JR Thorpe, "Can Anxiety Disorders Be Cured?," Bustle, May 9, 2016. www.bustle.com/articles/159598-can-anxiety-disorders-be-cured.

CHAPTER FIVE: MORE TO LEARN

18. Madeline R. Vann, "Is Anxiety Hereditary?," *Everyday Health*, August 24, 2015. www.everydayhealth.com/news/is-anxiety-hereditary/.

19. Bret Steka, "Can Fear Be Erased?," *Scientific American*, December 4, 2014. www.scientificamerican.com/article/can-fear-be-erased/.

20. Quoted in "Anxious Parents Can Transmit Anxiety to Children, Twin Study Shows," *Psychiatric News Alert*, April 27, 2015. alert.psychnews.org/2015/04/anxious-parents-can-transmit-anxiety-to.html.

21. Kyle Hill, "What Is a Good Study?: Guidelines for Evaluating Scientific Studies," *Science-Based Life*. sciencebasedlife.wordpress.com/resources-2/what-is-a-good-study-guidelines-for-evaluating-scientific-studies/.

22. "Scientific Studies: Last Week Tonight with John Oliver (HBO)," YouTube video, 19:27, posted by LastWeekTonight, May 8, 2016. www.youtube.com/watch?v=0Rnq1NpHdmw.

GLOSSARY

agoraphobia: Fear of being in a helpless or embarrassing situation in a public place.

anxiety disorder: A general term for a group of mental disorders in which severe anxiety is a major symptom.

clinical trial: A detailed investigation of a drug, a treatment, or a surgical device on consenting human subjects.

diabetes: A disease in which the blood's glucose, or sugar, levels are too high.

DNA: Deoxyribonucleic acid, a material that carries genetic instructions for all living things.

electroencephalogram (EEG): A graphic record of electrical activity in the brain.

enzyme: A protein that originates in living cells.

flashback: A vivid recollection of a traumatic event.

functional magnetic resonance imaging (fMRI): Medical test that uses radio waves to measure blood flow in the brain in order to see which parts of the brain are most active.

generalized anxiety disorder (GAD): An anxiety disorder characterized by an overall anxious mood with chronic anxiety symptoms, such as sweating and lightheadedness.

genetic engineering: The use of scientific methods and technology to manipulate or alter genetic material from one organism and to introduce the result into another organism in order to change one or more of its characteristics.

genetic marker: A readily recognizable genetic trait, gene, DNA segment, or gene product that enables tracking of specific genetic traits.

hallucination: When the mind creates a realistic experience that is not actually occurring.

hormone: A natural substance that is produced in the body and that influences the way the body grows or develops.

hyperglycemia: A high amount of glucose in the blood's plasma.

insomnia: Trouble falling asleep or staying asleep.

monoamine oxidase inhibitor (MAOI): One of a group of antidepressant drugs that increase the concentration of monoamines in the brain.

neurotransmitter: A chemical that relays signals to the brain.

norepinepherine: A neurotransmitter associated with alertness that is produced in response to a stressful situation.

obsessive-compulsive disorder (OCD): A disorder characterized by repetitive thoughts and actions taken in the hopes of stopping the thoughts.

panic attack: A sudden period of extreme anxiety.

panic disorder: An anxiety disorder characterized by repeated periods of extreme anxiety and fear, as well as persistent fear about when the next attack will occur.

post-traumatic stress disorder (PTSD): A psychological disorder caused by traumatic events.

selective serotonin reuptake inhibitor (SSRI): One of a class of drugs most often used in the treatment of depression and anxiety.

serotonin: A neurotransmitter involved with maintaining mood balance.

specific phobia: The most common anxiety disorder, characterized by irrational fear of an activity, object, or situation.

therapy: Meeting with a therapist to treat psychological disorders. Also, any treatment for a disorder.

tricylic antidepressant (TCA): One of an older group of antidepressants used in the treatment of depression and some anxiety disorders.

virtual environment: A computer-generated, three-dimensional environment.

virtual reality (VR): A simulated environment created by a complex, three-part computer system.

ORGANIZATIONS TO CONTACT

Anxiety and Depression Association of America (ADAA)
8701 Georgia Avenue
Suite 412
Silver Spring, MD 20910
www.adaa.org
Instagram: anxietyanddepression_adaa
ADAA is a nonprofit organization dedicated to educating both professionals and the public about anxiety disorders and treatment and helping people find treatment programs in their communities. It conducts monthly webinars and provides reference information on research.

Mental Health America
500 Montgomery Street
Suite 820
Alexandria, VA 22314
www.mentalhealthamerica.net
Instagram: mentalhealthamerica
YouTube: mentalhealthamerica
This organization's mission is to educate the public about mental health, fight for appropriate mental health care for all people, and provide support to people living with mental health issues or substance abuse problems.

National Alliance on Mental Illness (NAMI)
4301 Wilson Boulevard
Suite 300
Arlington, VA 22203
www.nami.org
Instagram: namicommunicate
TikTok: nami
YouTube: NAMICommunicate
NAMI is a national nonprofit outreach, educational, and advocacy organization dedicated to improving the lives of people with mental illnesses and their families.

National Institute of Mental Health (NIMH)
Office of Science Policy, Planning, and Communications
6001 Executive Boulevard, MSC 9663
Bethesda, MD 20892
www.nimh.nih.gov
Instagram: nimhgov
YouTube: NIMHgov
NIMH supports mental health in a number of ways. Hundreds of scientists and researchers conduct clinical trials supported by NIMH. The organization supports outreach programs and publishes educational materials in both English and Spanish. It also provides updates on the latest scientific developments in mental health.

National Social Anxiety Center
nationalsocialanxietycenter.com
This organization has 33 clinics across the United States where people can go to get help managing their social anxiety. Additionally, the website offers resources such as a quiz to see how severe a person's social anxiety is, a blog where other sufferers talk about their experiences, and self-help videos for people who are unable to see a therapist.

FOR MORE INFORMATION

BOOKS

Gross, Anouchka. *How to Manage Your Eco-Anxiety: An Empowering Guide for Young People.* New York, NY: Magic Cat Publishing, 2024.

Hemmen, Lucy. *The Teen Girl's Anxiety Survival Guide: 10 Ways to Conquer Anxiety and Feel Your Best.* Oakland, CA: Instant Help Books, 2021.

Lindsay, Toni. *Everything Anxiety Told You Is a Lie (*Well, Almost Everything!).* Chatswood, New South Wales, Australia: Exisle Publishing, 2024.

McDonagh, Thomas, and John Patrick Hatcher. *The Teen Anxiety Guidebook: Improve Self-Esteem, Discover New Coping Skills, and Relieve Social Anxiety, Worry, and Panic Attacks.* Berkeley, CA: Bloom Books for Young Readers, 2023.

Pedrick, Cherry, and Bruce M. Hyman. *More Than Just Stress: Understanding Anxiety Disorders.* Minneapolis, MN: Twenty-First Century Books, 2024.

WEBSITES

Anxiety Screening Quiz
psychcentral.com/quizzes/anxiety.htm
This quiz is not intended to diagnose an anxiety disorder, but it can help someone decide whether they should seek the advice of a doctor for diagnosis and treatment.

National Suicide Prevention Lifeline
1-800-273-8255
suicidepreventionlifeline.org
Sometimes people with anxiety disorders find life so difficult that they think about suicide. This hotline and its website provide emotional support to people who are in a difficult time in their life. The website has options to call, text, and chat online in both English and Spanish. It also offers video calls so people who are Deaf or hard of hearing can speak to someone in sign language.

Teen Talk
teentalkapp.org
This app is available for free on Android and iOS. It connects teens to each other and to professional counselors so they can talk about their mental health with like-minded and non-judgmental people.

INDEX

E

F

G

M

N

O

P

R

S

W

X

Y

Z

PHOTO CREDITS

Cover fizkes/Shutterstock.com; Cover, pp. 1, 3-112 Trisno Wardana/Shutterstock.com; Cover, pp. 1, 3, 4, 6, 10, 32, 48, 68, 81, 92, 96, 99, 101, 103, 111, 112 Sentavio/Shutterstock.com; p. 6 Nicoleta Ionescu/ Shutterstock.com; p. 8 https://commons.wikimedia.org/wiki/File:Charlotte_Bront%C3%AB.jpg; p. 11 Prostock-studio/Shutterstock.com; p. 13 Tero Vesalainen/Shutterstock.com; p. 16 New Africa/Shutterstock.com; p. 17 Djavan Rodriguez/ Shutterstock.com; p. 19 Jaguar PS/Shutterstock.com; p. 21 Debby Wong/Shutterstock.com; pp. 24, 45 fizkes/Shutterstock.com; p. 26, 29 Ground Picture/ Shutterstock.com; pp. 35, 55, 72 PeopleImages.com - Yuri A/Shutterstock.com; p. 38 Kateryna Onyshchuk/Shutterstock.com; p. 43 Rawpixel.com/Shutterstock.com; p. 49 Studio Romantic/ Shutterstock.com; p. 50 Drazen Zigic/Shutterstock.com; p. 53 Miguel Serrano Ruiz/Shutterstock.com; p. 58 shisu_ka/Shutterstock.com; p. 61 Studio Romantic/Shutterstock.com; p. 64 YARUNIV Studio/Shutterstock.com; p. 66 Miljan Zivkovic/ Shutterstock.com; p. 75 ORION PRODUCTION/ Shutterstock.com; p. 79 VH-studio/Shutterstock.com; p. 83 Egoreichenkov Evgenii/Shutterstock.com; p. 86 AnnaStills/Shutterstock.com.

ABOUT THE AUTHOR

AMY HOLT graduated from UCLA in 1997 with a degree in journalism. However, she soon realized she preferred the flexibility and freedom of freelancing. She began writing books for young adults and children in the early 2000s. In her spare time, Amy enjoys watching *Law and Order*, traveling to new places, and exploring public libraries.